Sout
Lakeland

Norman Buckley

Following more than forty years as a frequent visitor, Norman Buckley has lived in the Lake District since 1990, indulging his enthusiasm for this unique area, its history and its landscape.

For the last ten years he has been a prolific writer of guide books of different kinds; this is his sixth Lake District book, following the comprehensive "Landmark Visitors Guide to the Lake District" and several walking guides.

In partnership with his wife June, Norman has also written several books linking recommended walks and tea shops in various parts of Britain, with diplomas in Environmental Management and in Lake District Studies from the Universities of Liverpool and Lancaster respectively.

Acknowledgement

To my wife June, who not only contributed the sections on Accommodation, Eating Out and Beatrix Potter, but also provided a great deal of wide-ranging support throughout the whole period of the research and writing of this book.

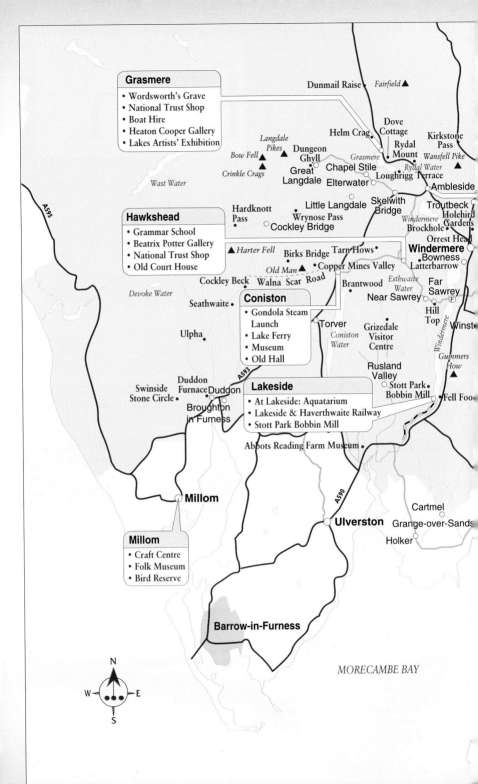

Grasmere
- Wordsworth's Grave
- National Trust Shop
- Boat Hire
- Heaton Cooper Gallery
- Lakes Artists' Exhibition

Dunmail Raise   *Fairfield* ▲

Langdale Pikes   Dungeon Ghyll   Helm Crag   Dove Cottage   Rydal Mount   Kirkstone Pass

Bow Fell ▲   *Grasmere*   *Wansfell Pike* ▲

Crinkle Crags ▲   Great Langdale   Chapel Stile   *Rydal Water*   Loughrigg Terrace

West Water   Elterwater ○   Ambleside

Little Langdale   Skelwith Bridge   Troutbeck   Holehird Gardens

Hardknott Pass   Wrynose Pass   *Windermere*   Brockhole

Hawkshead
- Grammar School
- Beatrix Potter Gallery
- National Trust Shop
- Old Court House

○ Cockley Bridge   Orrest Head

▲ *Harter Fell*   Birks Bridge   Tarn Hows •   **Windermere**

Old Man ▲ • Copper Mines Valley   •Bowness

Cockley Beck   Walna Scar Road   Brantwood   *Esthwaite Water*   Latterbarrow

Devoke Water   Seathwaite •   Near Sawrey ○   Far Sawrey

Ulpha .

Coniston
- Gondola Steam Launch
- Lake Ferry
- Museum
- Old Hall

Torver   Grizedale Visitor Centre   Hill Top   Winst

Coniston Water   *Gummers How* ▲

Rusland Valley   ○ Stott Park Bobbin Mill

Swinside Stone Circle •   Duddon Furnace   Duddon •   Broughton in Furness

Lakeside
- At Lakeside: Aquatarium
- Lakeside & Haverthwaite Railway
- Stott Park Bobbin Mill

• Fell Foo

Abbots Reading Farm Museum •

Millom
- Craft Centre
- Folk Museum
- Bird Reserve

○ **Millom**

Cartmel ○
Ulverston   Grange-over-Sands

Holker ○

Barrow-in-Furness

MORECAMBE BAY

N
W — E
S

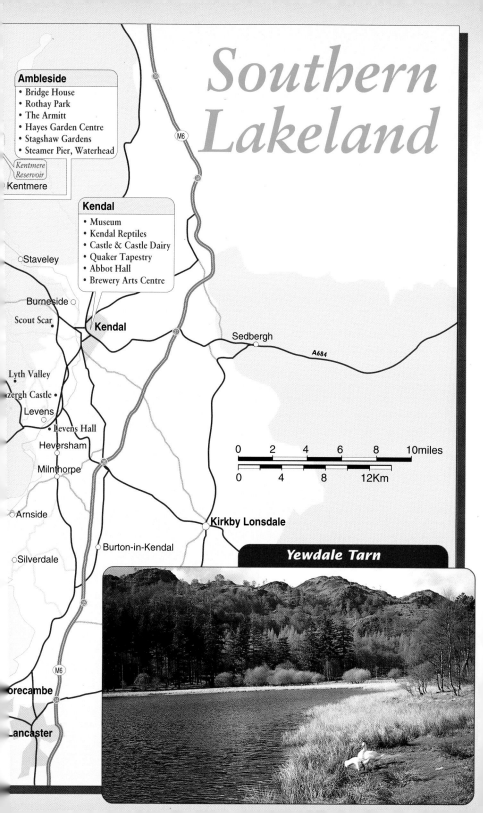

Southern Lakeland

Ambleside
- Bridge House
- Rothay Park
- The Armitt
- Hayes Garden Centre
- Stagshaw Gardens
- Steamer Pier, Waterhead

Kentmere Reservoir

Kentmere

Kendal
- Museum
- Kendal Reptiles
- Castle & Castle Dairy
- Quaker Tapestry
- Abbot Hall
- Brewery Arts Centre

M6

Staveley

Burneside

Scout Scar

Kendal

Sedbergh

A684

Lyth Valley

zergh Castle

Levens

Levens Hall

Heversham

Milnthorpe

Arnside

Kirkby Lonsdale

Burton-in-Kendal

Silverdale

| 0 | 2 | 4 | 6 | 8 | 10miles |
| 0 | 4 | 8 | 12Km |

M6

recambe

Lancaster

Yewdale Tarn

CONTENTS

Opposite: The quay at Coniston. The steamboat 'Gondola' calls her

Southern
Lakeland

Norman Buckley

Introduction

The Lake District is one of the most popular areas for visitors in this country. In all seasons, people come to explore its fells and valleys, whether in spring when wild daffodils may be seen in many areas, in the balmy days of summer, or autumn when the changing foliage brings a richness of the colours of the fells and lakes. Even in winter, a dusting of snow on the fells creates scenes of memorable beauty.

In addition to the fells, valleys and lakes, there are the literary attractions which draw visitors from all around the world who come in large numbers to see for themselves the homes of Beatrix Potter and William Wordsworth.

There is much to see and much to do, all of it set against a backdrop of magnificent scenery protected by the National Park and the area's major landowner, the National Trust. The Lake District attracts visitors back time and time again, often several times a year. The Lakeland experience endears and endures despite the passage of the years.

Yes, there is always a welcome in the Lake District, to new visitors and old friends alike. Even if it pours down while you are there, your enthusiasm to return will not be dampened. In that sense, the Lake District can readily claim to be the complete holiday destination.

This pocket guide does not pretend to provide a detailed introduction to the Lake District, its geology, history, landscape, flora and fauna, architecture and customs; many more substantial books are available to provide for the interests of visitors in these and other specialised subjects, whilst general guides such as the Landmark Visitors Guide to the Lake District include a substantial overall summary.

Suffice it to say that within the area's small compass of approximately 50km x 50km is packed more varied and spectacular scenery than anywhere else in Britain, including England's only true mountain area. The geology and the continuing human history, from the makers of the stone axes in Great Langdale through Romans, Vikings, Normans, wool-producing farmers, bobbin and gunpowder manufacturers, literary figures and painters, are never less than fascinating.

Largely because of the easy access by road and rail, the part of the Lake District covered by this book is undoubtedly the most popular. It encompasses all the features mentioned above, with an overlay of tourism which gives year-round life and activity to the towns and villages, with the consequent provision of a high proportion of the District's visitor attractions. It follows that the area is well provided with overnight accommodation, cafés and restaurants.

Not to be overlooked, of course, is that this bustling and attractive holiday area also has its share of the scenery, that wonderful blend of lakes, woodlands and mountains, which makes the Lake District as a whole so special.

EVENTS

KENDAL, AND STAVELEY

Westmorland County Show
Lane Farm, Crooklands, near Kendal. Comprehensive agricultural show with lots of events. Second week in September. ☎ 015395 67804

Lake District Sheepdog Trials
Ings near Staveley. Early August. ☎ 015394 33721

WINDERMERE

Lakes Summer Music
Occupying most of the first two weeks each August, this festival is held at several venues throughout South Lakeland, including the excellent hall at the school at Troutbeck Bridge, less than 2km (1.25 miles) along the main A591 Ambleside road. ☎ 01539 733411

Windermere Powerboat Record Attempts
Mid October. Low Wood Hotel (see above).

AMBLESIDE

Ambleside Daffodil and Spring Flower Show
Mid March. Details from Tourist Information Centre.

Ambleside Rush-bearing
St Mary's Church. First Saturday in July. Ceremonial renewal of the rushes which covered the earth floor in medieval times. ☎ 015394 33205

Ambleside Sports
Rydal Park, by the A591 Grasmere and Keswick road, just north of the town centre. Includes traditional Lake District events. Late July/early August. ☎ 015394 45531

Ambleside Flower Show and Craft Fair
Rugby Club, Borrans Road. Early August. ☎ 015394 32252

RYDAL

Rydal Sheepdog Trials
Ambleside showground field. Early/mid August.

GRASMERE

Grasmere Sports
On the large field adjacent to the main public car park/coach park. Largest and most popular of the traditional Lake District sports days, with a very comprehensive programme of events, including hound trailing and Cumberland and Westmorland wrestling. Held on the third Thursday after the first Monday in August. ☎ 015394 32127

Grasmere Rush-bearing
St Oswald's Church. Held on the Saturday nearest to St Oswald's Day (5 August). Rush-bearing goes back to the days when churches had earth floors, made more tolerable by a covering of rushes, which were ceremonially renewed each year.

Lakes Artists Exhibition
The Hall, Grasmere. Open daily late July–early September each year.

LANGDALE

Langdale Show
Traditional Lakeland country show held in mid August.

CONISTON

Coniston Water Festival
Late May and late July/early August. ☎ 015394 41707

HAWKSHEAD

Hawkshead Show
Hawkshead Hall Farm. Mid August. ☎ 015394 36609

LOWICK

Lowick Show
Early September.
☎ 015394 36364

BROUGHTON IN FURNESS

Millom and Broughton Show
West Park, Broughton in Furness. Late August.
☎ 01229 772556

1 Kendal & Staveley

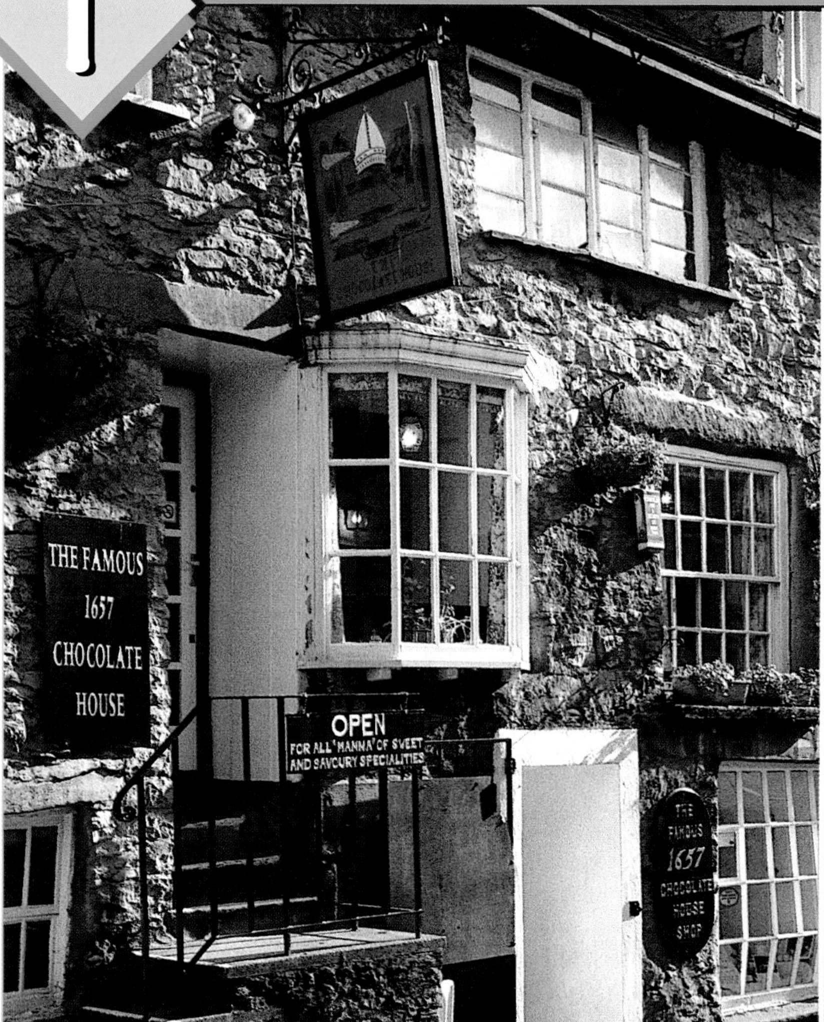

• KENDAL •

For the great majority of visitors, Kendal has long been the 'Gateway to the Lake District', although this is less apparent nowadays with the bypass whizzing motorists well away from the crowded streets of this bustling old town.

Standing astride the River Kent, **Kendal** is an ancient market town situated in a basin several kilometres south-east of the mountains of the Lake District proper, but with more gentle hills to the north, east and west. Immediately to the west, Scout Scar and Cunswick Scar, both facing away from the town, display some of the best surviving features of the limestone which once covered the whole district.

The strong north-south axis of the town, with the main street, named from the south, Kirkland, Highgate and Stricklandgate, well over one kilometre (three-quarters of a mile) in length, is a reminder of the communications importance of the town from Roman times, when there was a fort at Watercrook, just to the south. The main road to Scotland, first a turnpike road, then becoming the A6, was along this main street. Later came the main railway line from London to Glasgow, which passes a little way to the east, with a junction at Oxenholme. Last came the modern M6 motorway, again passing to the east of Kendal as it heads for the Lune Gorge and Shap as the easiest crossing of the high moorland.

The consistent use of local stone for the buildings gives Kendal a uniform, though at times rather dull, appearance – hence the nickname 'Old Grey Town'. As would be expected in the centre of an ancient barony, there is a medieval **castle** (of about 1180), its ruins standing high on a knoll to the east of the town centre from which it is not visible.

Kendal Castle

Easily reached from Aynam Road via Parr Street and Sunnyside and a short uphill walk, or from Castle Road and a longer walk. Unrestricted access as public footpaths cross the site. Fine views over the town. Street parking only.

This is in fact Kendal's second castle. An earlier structure, probably of wood, stood on another elevated site, which can still be identified to the west of the main street. One owner of the present castle was the father of Catherine Parr, the sixth wife of King Henry VIII.

The town itself grew from two early settlements, one around the present **Market Place** and the other some distance to the south by the **parish church**. The two later coalesced.

Market Place

Small but attractively animated when the street market is held each Wednesday and Saturday. Adjacent is the Westmorland Centre, a modern shopping complex which includes a daily indoor market. Across the Market Place is the Shambles, an attractive little street, formerly the trading place of the town's butchers.

Very distinctive in the development were the many close-knit residential 'yards' reached through narrow openings off the main streets. Claims that the tight packing of these small dwellings was for defensive protection against Scottish raiders are unfounded, as construction was long after hostilities had ceased. As in northern industrial towns generally, it was advantageous to pack as many workers as possible close to the mills and factories, in Kendal's case largely along the banks of the adjacent river. Many numbered yard entrances can still be seen but the houses were demolished and cleared, as having proper sanitation became obligatory.

Holy Trinity Parish Church

Mostly 18th century but standing on the site of an older church, this fine structure is found in Kirkland, close to the Abbot Hall. Reputed to be the largest parish church in the county, the width is particularly striking.

Inside Holy Trinity is the Parr Chapel, a memorial to Romney and the helmet and sword of 'Robert the Devil'. This character was Robert Phillipson of Belle Isle, Windermere who, during the Civil War, in pursuit of his Parliamentarian enemy Colonel Briggs, rode his horse into the church during a service, creating a fair amount of mayhem. Phillipson just about escaped with his life as the Parliamentarian congregation reacted violently, but lost his helmet, since displayed for all to see.

As an industrial town, Kendal has long been famous for woollens, carpets and other textiles, (there is a reference in William

Shakespeare's King Henry IV part I to knaves dressed in Kendal Green clothing), tobacco and snuff, leather goods (there is a present-day shoe industry) and water turbines.

Fortunately, many of the better old buildings have survived, at least in a modified form, largely along the main street where, above the mainly modern shop frontages, some fine old structures are apparent.

Castle Dairy

Wildman Street. The oldest occupied house in Kendal. The name may be a corruption of 'Castle Dowry' as it was believed to have been given by Sir Thomas Parr of Kendal Castle to his daughter Agnes as part of her dowry when she married his steward in about 1455. Originally a hall-house of the 14th century, it was extensively modified in the 16th century but many fine traditional structural features remain. Inside are the arms of both the Parr and the Strickland families. Inside viewing may be possible.

There are several old inns. For those with an hour or two to spare, Kendal lends itself well to the 'town trail' approach; two admirable *Discover Kendal* leaflets published by the Civic Society are available at a small charge at the Tourist Information Centre.

The Westmoreland Centre, Kendal

Abbot Hall

The Abbot Hall Art Gallery, situated in a Georgian mansion by the river, and the Museum of Lakeland Life and Industry on an adjacent site, are jointly administered. This highly regarded complex has first-class permanent collections, supplemented from time to time by visiting exhibitions. The Gallery is strong on Cumbrian painters, including locally born George Romney. Open 15 February–24 December, seven days a week, 10.30–17.00, but with earlier closing time of 16.00 in February, March, November and December. Admission Charge. Car Park. Coffee Shop. ☎ 01539 722464; fax 01539 722494.

Kentmere

The one-way traffic system in Kendal is notorious and is likely to be perplexing to visitors. Broadly, with clock-wise circulation, the system forms an elongated north-south oval, with a one-way cut across in the middle at Lowther Street, by the side of the town hall. Most of the car parks are towards the northern end of the town.

Kendal Museum

Station Road. A long established museum, Natural history, archaeology, and a special collection relating to the life and work of the celebrated local hill-walker and writer Alfred Wainwright. Admission charge; car park. ☎ 01539 721374. Open April to October 10.30–17.00, November to March 10.30–16.00, Monday to Saturday.

As befits a country centre with a considerable catchment area, the town is well provided with shops both traditional and modern. Unlike the smaller settlements in the Lake District proper, there are relatively few of the more gimmicky gift, Lakeland wool and so-called 'factory clothing' shops.

Situated to the north of Kendal is **Burneside**. It is an industrial settlement by the River Kent dominated by the large paper factory of James Cropper & Co.

There is a railway station on the Windermere branch line and Carus Green Golf Course is close by. Burneside Old Hall has more recent buildings grafted on to a 14th-century pele tower.

MORE PLACES TO VISIT
• Kendal •

Kendal Reptiles
117 Stricklandgate. Entrance to this small unusual attraction is through Hall's Pet Stores, just to the north of the junction with Sandes Avenue. Included is a snake nursery. ☎ 01539 721240

Friends Meeting House
Stramongate. An old Quaker site. Following a visit by George Fox in 1652, a first meeting house was opened here in 1688, followed by a school. The present building dates from 1815–16, designed for 850 people. The celebrated tapestry exhibition centre is open from spring to late autumn, Monday–Saturday, 10.00–17.00. Admission Charge. ☎ 01539 722975

Brewery Arts Centre
Highgate. By the side of the southern part of the main street, this former brewery has been tastefully converted into a multi-purpose centre, with theatrical productions, music, cinema and visiting exhibitions of various kinds. Café. Car Park (pay and display). ☎ 01539 725133

K Village
In recent years the ground floor of the K shoes factory in Lound Road has been converted into an assortment of tasteful shops specialising in factory 'seconds'. Included are Denby Ware, Van Heusen and K shoes. Café. Car Park. ☎ 01539 716648

Kendal Leisure Centre
Burton Road. By the side of the main road from Kendal to Oxenholme, Endmoor and Burton in Kendal, this modern multi-purpose sport and leisure complex offers swimming, sauna/solarium, fitness room, squash, badminton and other indoor sports. Concerts and occasional theatre are held on some evenings. Café. Bar. Car Park. ☎ 01539 29777; fax 01539 731135

Kendal Golf Club
Situated on high ground to the west of the town, accessed by Allhallows Lane and Beast Banks. Turn right into High Tenterfell and follow the signposts up to the left. Established golfers welcome as visitors. ☎ 01539 723499 (professional's shop).

Carus Green Golf Course
In the valley of the River Kent, almost at Burneside. Fork right from the A5284 Windermere road at the Methodist Chapel. The course is on the right in less than 2 km (1.25 miles). Pay and Play course. ☎ 01539 721097

• STAVELEY •

Between Kendal and Windermere on the A591 lies Staveley, a large village well equipped with shops and inns and with a considerable industrial history. The River Kent and its tributary the River Gowan formerly powered several mills making bobbins and processing textiles. The village, which has a railway station on the Windermere branch line, is much improved since the bypass was constructed a few years ago.

Woodcraft Workshop – Peter Hall & Son

Visitors can see craftsmen at work on a variety of new and antique furniture. Open throughout the year, Monday–Friday, 9.00–17.00; Saturday and Bank Holidays 10.00–16.00 (showroom only).

Upstream of Staveley the valley of Kentmere becomes progressively hemmed in by the mountains of the two arms of the Kentmere Horseshoe, rising to High Street.

Kentmere hamlet north of Staveley has the 15th-century church of St Cuthbert and the Old Hall nearby, a 14th-century pele tower incorporated into more modern farm buildings.

The River Kent at Staveley

1 ↑ ● ● ● Scout Scar

Easy, almost level walk with wonderful views. Optional length — typically 3km (2 miles)

By car, from the main street in Kendal turn left into Allhallows Lane, at the traffic lights directly opposite the town hall; continue up Beast Banks, soon forking right into Greenside. Heading for Underbarrow and Crosthwaite, the road climbs out of town to cross the main bypass. In about 2km (1.25 miles) from the town centre the signposted car park is in a former quarry on the right.

Walk across the road, go through an old metal gate and ascend quite steeply to the right to reach the top of the scar. The length of the walk is now optional, the long flat top extending to the south for several kilometres. Make your own circuit. Most people head for the prominent shelter building, where a rather worn frieze sets out the highlights of the view which is the crowning glory of this pleasant little walk. To the south is the estuary of the River Kent, merging into Morecambe Bay, with the knoll of Arnside Knott beyond. To the west and north a great panoply of Lake District mountains beckons, with the Langdale Pikes as the most instantly recognisable, whilst away to the east the long chain of the Pennine Hills includes the Howgill Fells above Sedbergh and the well-known peak of Ingleborough.

As this walk is on limestone, it is very dry underfoot and is one of the few walks in the district which does not really need proper walking boots.

2 ↑ ● ● ● Kentmere Reservoir

Almost level walk on good tracks. 8km (5 miles).

From the small car park at Kentmere hamlet continue along the surfaced road and keep right at a junction in 400m or so. Where the road ends, bypass Hartrigg Farm and continue along a good track beneath the steep slopes of Rainsborrow Crag to the reservoir at the head of the valley, a very pleasant spot ideal for family picnics.

Cross to the other side of the valley, either at the dam or about 400m downstream. The return path passes through the ruins of Tongue House; there is the site of an ancient settlement at the rear. At Overend Farm keep right to pass below Hallow Bank hamlet, continuing along a walled lane (Low Lane) which angles up to join a surfaced roadway (High Lane).

At the first road junction turn right, downhill, then right again to return to the car park.

Windermere & Bowness

2

Possibly the best known place name in the Lake District, Windermere can refer to either the lake or the large village which grew around the terminus of the railway line some 2km (1.25 miles) from the lake.

• WINDERMERE – THE LAKE •

The biggest lake in England at nearly 17km (10.5 miles) in length, Windermere is a fine sheet of water with numerous, mostly small, wooded islands. The only inhabited island is the largest, Belle Isle, close to Bowness, which has a villa dating from 1774, the first truly circular residence in Britain. There is no public access to Belle Isle.

From its southern end in comparatively low-lying countryside, the lake reaches close to high mountains at the north, the ring forming the **Fairfield Horseshoe** above Ambleside and Rydal providing a wonderful panorama. Along much of the west shore the well-wooded **Claiffe Heights** plunge steeply towards the water, whilst the gentler eastern shore has been more built up with individual residences and the settlements of **Bowness** and **Waterhead**.

The lake is extremely popular for boating, several thousand craft ranging from tiny dinghies to substantial cruisers being registered as users. Near the mid point is the **car ferry**, the modern vessel a successor to several more primitive ferries. Three hundred years ago a ferry sank with the loss of more than 30 lives. From the west side at **Ferry Nab** the road leads to

Brockhole

The comprehensive visitor centre of the Lake District National Park Authority, 3.5km (2 miles) along the A591 Ambleside road. Permanent exhibition; audio visual presentations; frequent events; large terraced garden; adventure playground; lake shore access; disabled access; gift and book shop; restaurant/tearoom. Free entry but charge for car parking. Open late March to end of October, 10.00–17.00 every day.
☎ 015394 46601;
fax 015394 45555

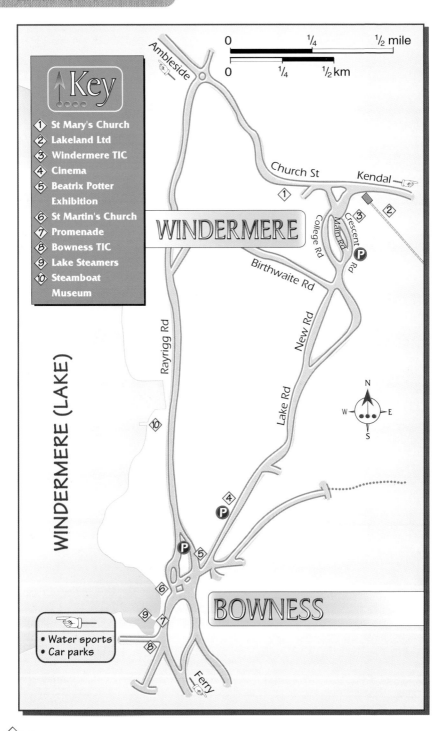

Far and Near Sawrey and Hawkshead.

Timetabled boat services ply between Lakeside, Bowness and Waterhead (for Ambleside), with some calls at Brockhole, the Lake District National Park Visitor Centre.

In season, attractive large diesel powered 'steamers' are used, the late 19th-century *Tern* being particularly elegant. In winter much reduced services are operated by smaller motor launches. In addition to the scheduled services, during high season there are frequent and varied circular trips from Bowness and Waterhead.

Fell Foot at the southern end of Windermere

Windermere Iron Steamboat Co. Ltd/Bowness Bay Boating Co. Ltd

Jointly operating from Lakeside: ☎ 015394 31188, fax 015395 31947; Bowness: ☎ 015394 43360 or 015394 43056, fax 015394 43468; and Waterhead: ☎ 015394 32225

At Lakeside, connections may be made with the steam-hauled trains of the Lakeside and Haverthwaite Railway, for which combined tickets may be purchased. A 'Freedom of the Lake' ticket allows unlimited cruising for a period of 24 hours, whilst a combined ticket for the boat and the Aquarium of the Lakes at Lakeside is also discounted.

Rowing and small motor boats are available for individual hire at Bowness and Waterhead. Water-skiing and similar sports may be pursued at the Low Wood Hotel, by the side of the main road to the south of Waterhead and at Sport Aquatic at Windermere Quays, Glebe Road, Bowness. Hire of yachts, with a skipper, is possible at the Spinnaker Club, Windermere Marina Village, 1km (0.6 mile) south of Bowness on the A592 road to Newby Bridge. At Shepherd's Boat Yard, Glebe Road, Bowness, cruises on a modern luxury cruiser *Spirit of the Lake* are available. This boat may also be chartered by the hour.

CRUISING & WATERSPORTS

Low Wood Hotel
By the A591 on the way
to Waterhead. Waterskiing
and other lake sports.
☎ 015394 33338

Maples Yachting
Marina Village,
near Bowness.
☎ 0589 773292

Shepherd's Boatyard
Glebe Road, Bowness.
Luxury cruises on *Spirit of
the Lake,* Speedboat rides.
☎/fax 015394 48322

Sport Aquatic
Waterski school.
Windermere Visitor Centre,
Glebe Road, Bowness Bay.
☎ 015394 42121

**Water Activities at
Windermere,
Lake Holidays Afloat**
Glebe Road, behind
Ship Inn, Bowness Bay.
Hire of motor and
sailing boats
(instruction available)
Waterski school.
Open all year.
☎ 015394 43415

**Windermere
Outdoor Adventure
Watersports Centre**
Operated by South Lakeland
District Council on the
eastern shore of the lake
about 1km (0.6 mile) north
of Bowness village. Courses
in dinghy sailing, canoeing,
windsurfing etc. Open mid-
March to end November,
09.00–17.00 daily.
☎ 015394 47183

*Windermere is very popular
for watersports*

Most important is the **Windermere Ferry**, which for centuries has crossed the lake at a narrow part between the landing stage just to the south of Bowness and Ferry Nab. The present vessel is fixed to a submerged chain, plying to and fro every 20 minutes from 07.00 until 22.00 in summer, but terminating at 21.00 in winter. Eighteen average size vehicles are carried each journey, together with foot passengers. Services are suspended in very windy weather. The ferry is operated on behalf of Cumbria County Council.

• WINDERMERE - THE VILLAGE •

Windermere's village is basically a 19th-century settlement of rather austere solid stone buildings, with a small shopping centre and several inns and restaurants. There is a large car park for shoppers at Booth's supermarket and a pay and display public car park in Broad Street.

The **Railway station** is the terminus of the branch line from Oxenholme and still an important access to the district. Much of the original station is now incorporated into the adjacent supermarket.

PLACES TO VISIT
• Windermere Village •

Lakeland Ltd
On former railway land beside the station, this trading enterprise (formerly Lakeland Plastics), with its comprehensive array of kitchen and other domestic equipment has developed into a substantial visitor attraction.
Café. Open daily, including Sundays and Bank Holidays.
☎ 015394 88100

Tourist Information Office
Well situated between the railway station and the village, at the junction of the main A591 and High Street.
☎ 015394 46499

Baddeley Clock
By the roadside half way to Bowness is this monument erected in 1907 in memory of M.J.B. Baddeley, author of noted guide books.

Windermere Golf Club
Cleabarrow. Long established club with sporting upland course. Established golfers welcome as visitors.
☎ 015394 43550 (professional)

• BOWNESS ON WINDERMERE •

Although it is very much the holiday part of the Windermere/Bowness built-up area, with a good deal of modern development, ironically Bowness claims what is much the oldest portion of the settlement. The narrow streets clustered behind St Martin's parish church include buildings 300 years or more old; many houses were lived in by boatmen or fishermen.

St Martin's Church

Built in 1483. The east window includes glass believed to have been brought from Cartmel Priory following the Dissolution in 1539. Wooden statue of St Martin. Old font. 19th-century restoration has resulted in a light and bright interior. Not always open.

including speedboat racing, on the lake. Pride of place goes to the collection of lovely old steam launches, evocative of the late 19th and early 20th centuries, when the families living in the recently built gracious houses nearby would steam around the lake either individually or as part of the frequent regattas, as a favourite leisure activity.

Windermere Steamboat Museum

Steam launch trips in season. Model boat rally (two-day event) during the second week in May. Annual steamboat association rally in late July. Frequent small art exhibitions; museum shop; disabled access; light refreshments; picnic area.
Open daily from Easter to October, 10.00–17.00.
☎ 015394 45565

The large number of shops includes a high proportion catering for visitors and there are inns and restaurants to suit virtually all tastes. Worth a special mention is the very old Hole in t'Wall, formerly the New Hall Inn, tucked away in the old part of the village.

About 1km (0.6 mile) from the centre of Bowness, along Rayrigg Road, is the **Windermere Steamboat Museum**, an attractive modern museum, on the lake shore, displaying the history of boating,

By the lake shore, the promenade is a bustling place in high season, with all kinds of boating activity contributing to the holiday atmosphere. The characteristic boatmen's huts, replacements of 19th-century structures, are known locally as 'cushion huts'.

Sitting high above the promenade is the Belsfield Hotel, one of the early mansions built in a commanding position to provide fine views over the lake. The second owner, in the later part of the 19th century, was the industrialist H.W. Schneider, whose wealth was founded on iron, steel and armaments at Barrow in Furness.

Each day Schneider walked down through the garden to his waiting steam launch, *Esperance* . His butler followed close behind with breakfast on a silver tray, for consumption during the sail down the lake to Lakeside. Here a private train (Schneider was a director of the Furness Railway Company) took the great man on to his business at Barrow.

Car parking. Small – Crag Brow near the cinema. Large – Rayrigg Road (short and long stay sections). Largest – follow Glebe Road, passing a small car park, to reach Braithwaite Fold, near the caravan site; some way from the village, but served in season by a 'road train'.

Bowness, where you can take a leisurely cruise to Lakeside (to the south) or Waterhead (Ambleside)

MORE PLACES TO VISIT

Royalty Cinema,
Crag Brow (the main road towards Windermere village).
Three screens. Up-to-date films.
☎ 015394 43364

Beatrix Potter Experience
Crag Brow. A fairly recent conversion of a large old laundry building into two visitor attractions. The first is a small, versatile **theatre** offering occasional productions of high quality, exhibitions and some musical events. The autumn festival of theatre and music features artists of international repute.

The World of Beatrix Potter is a series of animated tableaux depicting the animals created by the great children's writer, supported by audio-visual displays and shop. Tearoom with light meals. Open every day apart from Christmas Day and the occasional shutdown for refurbishment of the exhibits.

Open: Easter to the end of September 10.00 to 1830, October to Easter 10.00 to 16.00.
☎ 015394 88444

The "World of Beatrix Potter" attraction at Bowness is a favourite with adults & children

• Bowness •

Tourist Information Centre
Centrally situated near the boat landings.
Includes Countryside Theatre with talks
and audio-visual displays.
☎ 015394 42895

**Public Tennis Courts and Pitch
and Put Golf Course**
Glebe Road. Booking at hut behind
Tourist Information Centre.

Amazonia, World of Reptiles
Windermere Quays Visitor Centre,
Bowness Bay. Extensive collection
of snakes, lizards, amphibians and
insects in botanical gardens.
Some animals for purchase.
Open Monday to Saturday 09.00–
18.00, Sunday 11.00–18.00, daily
except Christmas Day and New Year's
Day. ☎ 015394 48002

*The Steamboat
Museum, near Bowness*

View from the top of Brant Fell towards Waterhead

WALKS

1 Orrest Head

2.25km (1.5 miles). A very short but quite steep little walk, often a revelation for first time visitors as the views from the top, at 239m (784 feet), include much of the glory of southern Lakeland.

Cross the main A591 road close to the NatWest bank in Windermere. A signboard points the way along a broad, surfaced roadway, rising steeply as it weaves around substantial properties. There is soon a view of the lake. With more open country on the right, the surfaced road ends at Ellerey Wood Cottage. Continue along a broad, stony track, straight across at a junction of paths, now more level and possibly muddy.

Bend right along the side of a wall to rise again towards the summit, now visible to the left, above. Go left through a kissing-gate to reach the summit, where identification of the mountains is helped by a view board.

Return to the kissing-gate and down by the wall. Return either by the same route or make a circular walk as follows. By an arrowed post leave the outward route by continuing down by the wall to meet another track. Turn left, then right at another yellow arrow, along a broad, unsurfaced track, descending more gently.

Masses of wild rhododendron cover this hillside. Go right as the track forks, bear left at a junction by a high stone wall, and rejoin the surfaced road, turning right to go back to the village.

Orrest Head near Winderemere. There are wonderful views across Windermere from here.

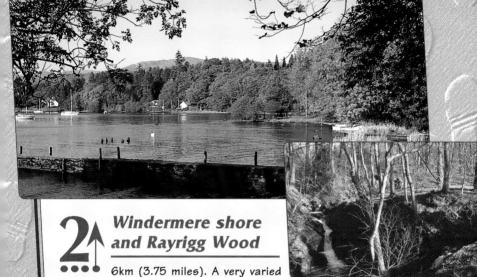

2 ⬆ *Windermere shore and Rayrigg Wood*

•••• ⬆ 6km (3.75 miles). A very varied short walk combining woodland with a very attractive section of lake shore. Views across the lake to Claiffe Heights.

Top: Low Millerground on Windermere in autumn
Above: Sherrif's Walk in Rayrigg Wood in Winter

From Crag Brow in Bowness, set off down Longlands Road, close to the cinema. Bear right to pass the rugby club and continue along the broad track into and through the woods, ignoring any side tracks. Emerge at Beemire Road, soon reaching Birthwaite Road. Turn left, then right at a signposted footpath. Follow this path to the main A591, reached close to St Mary's Church.

Turn left, then left again at once into another signposted path. Stay with this path as it descends steadily to Rayrigg Road. Cross the road to a gate and continue down by the side of an attractively rushing stream to the lake shore at Low Millerground, the site of a ferry many years ago. The housing for the call bell can still be seen. Turn left and take the delightful lake shore path, soon passing the landing stages and barbecue/picnic area at Rayrigg.

As the path ends, turn left to cross a meadow, back to Rayrigg Road. The ancient Rayrigg Hall is to the right. Turn right at the road, and walk by the roadside towards Bowness. Close to the Steamboat Museum turn left up a broad roadway to rejoin Longlands Road. Turn right to return to Crag Brow.

• TROUTBECK •

North of Windermere lies Troutbeck. It is very much a linear village, a series of hamlets loosely strung together along the valley side well above the Trout Beck from which its name is derived. The best feature is the fine array of traditional vernacular Lakeland buildings, largely dating from the 17th century. Brunskill's *Vernacular Architecture of the Lake Counties* sets out a fascinating trail from one end of the village to the other, with detailed descriptions of more than 30 of these buildings. Included is one of the 'spinning galleries' in a building across the road from the post office stores.

There are two inns, one of which – the Mortal Man – has a famous sign. The views across the valley to the ridge, which from the right includes Yoke, Ill Bell and Froswick, are very fine.

Jesus Parish Church is on the site of an earlier church by the side of the main Windermere to Patterdale road (A592) in the valley bottom, the present structure dating from 1736, with restoration in the 19th and 20th centuries. The churchyard is noted for its daffodils. Inside, most notable is the large east window by the Pre-Raphaelite painter Edward Burne-Jones, allegedly assisted by his friends William Morris and Ford Maddox Brown who happened to be on a fishing holiday nearby at the time.

Townend

At the south end of Troutbeck village, a former 'statesmans' (yeoman farmer) house of 1626 which was the home of the Browne family for more than 300 years. Since 1943 in the care of the National Trust, the interior has been kept as it was during occupation by the family. Admission charge. Open late March to end of October, Tuesday to Friday, Sundays and Bank Holiday Mondays, 13.00–17.00. ☎ 015394 32628

Holehird Gardens

To the right of the Windermere to Patterdale road (A592) about 1km (0.6 mile) north of the mini roundabout on the fringe of Windermere village. Entered by a drive past an obvious lodge. Holehird is a grand house of the mid-19th century, twice rented as a summer holiday home by Beatrix Potter's family and now in use as a Cheshire Home. A large area of the garden has been taken over by the Lakeland Horticultural Society and is beautifully maintained by the members. The national collections of hydrangeas and astilbes are housed here. Open to visitors. Car Park. No charge, but donation requested.

Townend, now a National Trust property at Troutbeck

• AMBLESIDE •

Situated close by the River Rothay 1.5km (1 mile) from the north end of Windermere, the stone-built market town of Ambleside has a fine scenic backdrop of mountains. Understandably popular with visitors, but still a thriving community in winter, the town seems large by Lake District standards; its truly compact size can best be appreciated by climbing a little way up one of the surrounding hillsides.

The Bridge House, Ambleside

The oldest part of the town rises steeply to the east of the main street, from North Road by the Salutation, an old coaching inn, up to Smithy Brow and Chapel Hill, with narrow streets and old stonework making an attractive combination. **How Head**, close to the converted chapel, dates in part from the 15th century, and is almost certainly the oldest building in town.

Stock Ghyll, a tributary of the River Rothay, tumbles down a famous waterfall, **Stock Ghyll Force**, signposted along the road behind the Salutation. The fall is just a few minutes walk away. Between the foot of the fall and the town centre was an impressive array of water-powered mills, which produced bobbins, processed fabrics and ground corn. Although the mills are long closed and most have been demolished or converted, the view from the main street bridge upstream along the beck still gives some impression of those industrial days.

Bridge House

A curious little structure which has graced a million post cards, bestriding Stock Beck by the side of the main road. Formerly the apple store to Ambleside Hall. Houses a **National Trust information centre** and small shop.

The modern town has many shops, both for basic needs and for visitor requirements. Particularly plentiful are those selling climbing, mountain walking and general outdoor activity clothing and gear. Similarly, there is no shortage of inns, cafés and restaurants. The combination of cinema, vegetarian restaurant and mini-shopping arcade at **Zeffirelli's** in Compston Road is unique in Lakeland.

All in all, Ambleside is a pleasant place in which to wander. Many will continue, either on foot or by car (a horse and trap operates from the town centre in season), along Lake Road or Borrans Road to **Waterhead** at the lakeside, an outpost where hotels and boat landings contribute to the holiday atmosphere. The steamer pier (☎ 015394 32225) is the northern terminus of the scheduled services. Close by are lakeside **Stagshaw Gardens** and the 1st-century Roman fort of **Galava**.

The Armitt

Just beyond Bridge House. Esteemed local history library and collection, recently expanded into an interactive exhibition of Lakeland life and times. Natural history watercolours by Beatrix Potter. Gift shop. Admission charge. Open all year, daily 10.00–17.00.
☎ 015394 33949

Stagshaw Gardens

National Trust. Situated along the A591 Windermere road, 500m beyond the Waterhead traffic lights. Narrow turning to left, easily missed. Very much a spring garden, open to visitors 1 April to end of June, daily 10.00–18.30. No visitor facilities.

Galava

1st-century Roman fort on low-lying land by the head of the lake, beyond the lake-side gardens. National Trust. Foundations only.

The largest car park is by the side of the main A591 road to Grasmere and Keswick, just north of the town centre, opposite the attractive Charlotte Mason College, now part of St Martin's College, Lancaster. Smaller car parks are found in Kelsick Road, opposite the library, and off Lake Road just south of the Kelsick Road junction. Further out of town along Lake Road, there is usually space at Low Fold car park. Waterhead has its own large car park.

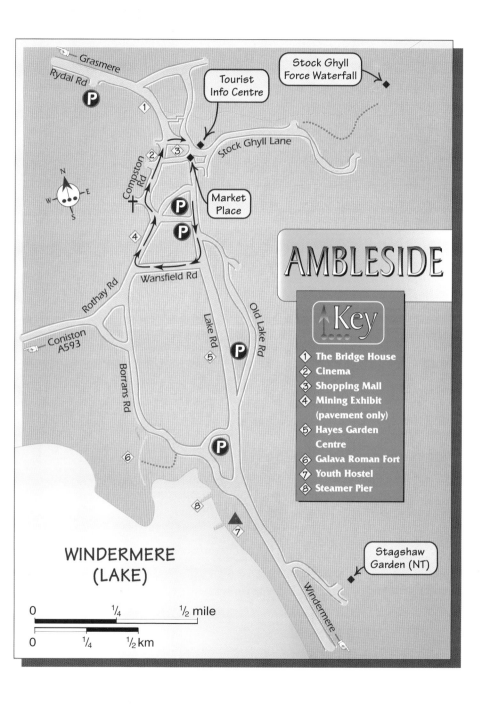

Grasmere

Rydal Rd

Tourist
Info Centre

Stock Ghyll
Force Waterfall

P

1

Compston Rd

2 3

Stock Ghyll Lane

N
W-E
S

Market
Place

P

P

4

Wansfield Rd

Rothay Rd

Lake Rd

5

Old Lake Rd

P

Coniston
A593

Borrans Rd

P

6

P

8

7

AMBLESIDE

Key

1 The Bridge House
2 Cinema
3 Shopping Mall
4 Mining Exhibit
   (pavement only)
5 Hayes Garden
   Centre
6 Galava Roman Fort
7 Youth Hostel
8 Steamer Pier

Stagshaw
Garden (NT)

WINDERMERE
(LAKE)

Windermere

0   ¼   ½ mile

0   ¼   ½ km

MORE PLACES TO VISIT
• Ambleside •

Old Stamp House
Church Street. Where William Wordsworth worked as Distributor of Stamps.

St Mary's Church
At the bottom end of Compston Road. 19th-century with spire, very unusual in Lakeland. Colourful mural of rush bearing and also sculpture by the celebrated Josefina de Vasconcellos, a local resident.

A quiet corner of Ambleside

Rothay Park
Large grassed areas behind the church, fine for picnics and children's play. Footpaths to the river.

Adrian Sankey
Glass-blowing workshop close to Bridge House. Café/restaurant. Open daily 09.00-17.30. ☎ 015394 33039

Bowls, Tennis, Putting
Public facilities beside the church.

Market
Very small. On car park in Kelsick Road, opposite the library. Wednesday.

Hayes Garden Centre
Lake Road. A considerable all-weather visitor attraction. ☎ 01539433434

Sail 'n' Dine
Jetty at Langdale Chase Hotel, on A591 1.5km (1 mile) south of Waterhead. Sailing with meals provided on board. End of March to end of October. Sailing tuition also available. ☎ 015242 74255; Yacht mobile: 0421 836 470

Tourist Information Centres
Ambleside, opposite new shopping mall. ☎ 015394 32582

Waterhead, Public car park
☎ 015394 32729

• RYDAL •

With a picturesque setting between the steep face of Nab Scar and the placid Rydal Water, the scattered village of Rydal is by the side of the A591 Ambleside to Grasmere and Keswick road. Were it not for Rydal Mount and Rydal Hall the village would scarcely warrant a mention. However, the small lake is very beautiful and there are attractive walks linking it with the better known Grasmere.

Rydal Mount

At the top of the no through road, a substantially extended old farmhouse rented and occupied by William Wordsworth and family from 1813 to 1850, the last 37 years of his life. Pleasant gardens and lake views. The house belongs to descendants of Wordsworth and contains some of his furniture and belongings. Car Park. Admission charge (reciprocal discounted tickets with Dove Cottage and Wordsworth House are available). Open March to October 09.30–17.00; November to February 10.00–16.00 (closed Tuesdays in winter). ☎ 015394 33002; fax 015394 31738.

Rydal Hall, a large building mostly of the 18th and 19th centuries, but with older portions was the home of the Le Fleming family for about 300 years and is now used as a conference and retreat centre by the Diocese of Carlisle. The house is not open to the public. The formal gardens were laid out by Thomas Mawson in 1909 and the parkland extends almost to Ambleside. There are large camping areas and a youth centre used by organisations such as Boy Scouts and Girl Guides.

Rydal Beck cascades through the grounds, with two good waterfalls; the oldest 'viewing house' in the country (1669) is carefully sited below the lower fall, but is not open to the public. This fall has been painted by many artists, including Joseph Wright of Derby. A right of way runs behind the house and on through the parkland and there is limited access to the gardens with sculpture by Josefina de Vasconcellos of Ambleside. A teashop can be found behind the house.

The start (or finish!) of the Fairfield Horseshoe mountain walk is at Rydal and a very good, but more modest, ramble is along the former 'coffin track', starting near Rydal Mount. (See walks).

MORE PLACES TO VISIT
• Rydal •

St Mary's Church
Built by Lady LeFleming of Rydal Hall in 1823, originally as a chapel – Wordsworth was a chapel warden. His family pew is at the front on the north side. Dr. Arnold and family, who lived nearby, had the opposite pew. The church was considered to be rather cramped and was enlarged in 1884.

Dora's Field
National Trust. Just behind the church, this piece of land was purchased by Wordsworth in 1826, when he was at risk of eviction from Rydal Mount. His intention was to build a house on the land. However, he stayed at Rydal Mount and later gave the land to his daughter Dora. The fine display of daffodils to be seen in spring was not the subject of the famous poem!

The River Rothay, Rydal

• GRASMERE •

A major and readily accessible visitor attraction, Grasmere village sits by the head of the lake in a broad vale at the foot of Dunmail Raise, where the main A591 road climbs over a low pass to Keswick. The village is overlooked by mountains. Silver Howe, the sharply pointed Helm Crag and Stone Arthur are most prominent, but the greater heights of Helvellyn and Fairfield are also close by.

Until comparatively recent times the vale was a centre of farming, mainly sheep, with a rural tranquillity which was highly acclaimed by the distinguished tourists of the 18th century. Thomas Gray, one of the earliest of these literary visitors, waxed eloquent – 'Not a single red tile, no flaring gentleman's house, or garden walls, break in upon the repose of this little unsuspected paradise; but all is peace, rusticity, and happy poverty in its neatest, most becoming attire'. Whether Gray had any evidence of the happiness or otherwise of those suffering the poverty is not recorded. Anyway, whilst the vale is still beautiful, Grasmere itself is now a much more sophisticated place, with tourism replacing farming as the main local occupation.

The village is large, with separate hamlets at Town End and Town Head, and is well served with shops, hotels and a small number of cafés/teashops. The lake is almost 1.5km (1 mile) in length, with a wooded island adding to its charm. Rowing boats may be hired from a site close to the village. Fittingly for a place

Sara Nelson's

A tiny shop close to the church, formerly the village school room. Gingerbread made to a secret recipe has been sold here since the middle of the 19th century.

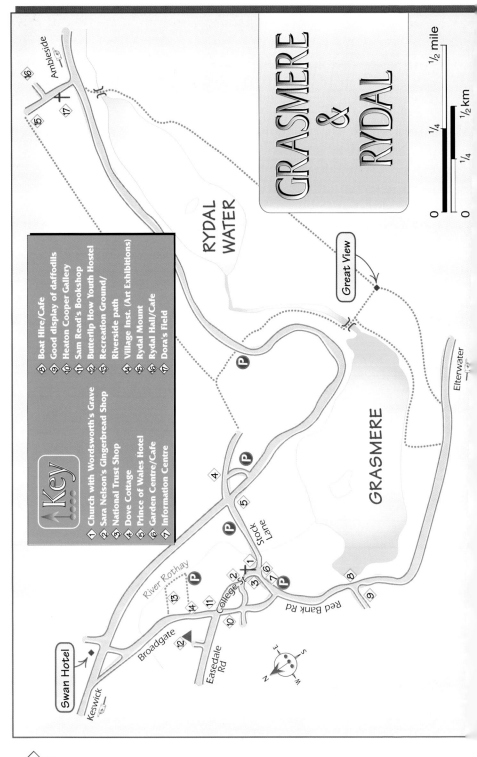

GRASMERE & RYDAL

Key

1. Church with Wordsworth's Grave
2. Sara Nelson's Gingerbread Shop
3. National Trust Shop
4. Dove Cottage
5. Prince of Wales Hotel
6. Garden Centre/Cafe
7. Information Centre
8. Boat Hire/Cafe
9. Good display of daffodils
10. Heaton Cooper Gallery
11. Sam Read's Bookshop
12. Butterlip How Youth Hostel
13. Recreation Ground/ Riverside path
14. Village Inst. (Art Exhibitions)
15. Rydal Mount
16. Rydal Hall/Cafe
17. Dora's Field

RYDAL WATER

Great View

GRASMERE

Swan Hotel

Keswick

Ambleside

Elterwater

Broadgate

Easedale Rd

River Rothay

College St

Stock Lane

Red Bank Rd

0   ¼   ½ km

0   ¼   ½ mile

which has so excited literary figures over the years, this is very much Wordsworth country, with three residences – **Dove Cottage** with its adjacent museum, the **Old Rectory** and **Allan Bank** – and his family grave all to be seen.

Dove Cottage was a former inn, the Dove and Olive Branch, at Town End hamlet on the east side of the A591 main road. It was the home of William, Mary and Dorothy Wordsworth from 1799 to 1808, when the increasing size of the family necessitated a move to larger accommodation. Much of William's best and most youthful work was done at Dove Cottage. and many of the great literary figures of the day, including Samuel Taylor Coleridge, Thomas De Quincey, Sir Walter Scott and Robert Southey, were hosted here. The cottage is still much the same as it was in Wordsworth's time and an agricultural building at the rear has been converted into a museum housing the William Wordsworth Trust's collection of manuscripts, books and paintings.

Dove Cottage and the Wordsworth Museum

Special exhibitions each year. Cottage and museum open to visitors daily 9.30–17.30, but some winter closing, usually mid January to mid February. Small car park. Shop. Admission charge, but reciprocal tickets with Rydal Mount and Wordsworth House (Cockermouth). ☎ 015394 35544 Tearoom open daily 10.00–17.00. Restaurant open Fridays, Saturdays and most evenings in season 18.30–21.30 (last orders), ☎ 015394 35268; fax 015394 35748

Likewise, it is hardly surprising that painters have also long had an interest in this rather special place. Two galleries now offer original works and, in one case, a large choice of prints for purchase.

A car and coach park is prominent by the southern entrance to the village. There are more car parks a little way along the road which turns off to the left, opposite the church, and at the far end of the village, beside the village hall.

Heaton Cooper Studio

Overlooking the central village green, a prominent gallery displaying and selling the work of several members of the Heaton Cooper family. Some original works but mainly prints of favourite Lakeland scenes, of various sizes and with choices of frame available. ☎ 015394 35280

MORE PLACES TO VISIT
• Grasmere •

St Oswald's Parish Church
In the village centre. Largely 13th and 14th centuries with later extensions. The rendered exterior is unprepossessing, but the interior is full of interest, not least the curious lop-sided effect brought about by enlargement, a memorial to William Wordsworth and a *Madonna and child* by Ophelia Gordon Bell, of the Heaton Cooper family. The Words-worth family grave and that of Hartley Coleridge are at the rear of the churchyard.

Old Rectory
Opposite the church. Home of the Wordsworths from 1811 to 1813, a very unhappy time as two of their children died during this period, and the house itself was not very satisfactory, being cold and damp. Not open to the public.

National Trust Shop
Across the road from the gingerbread shop.

Tourist Information Office
Tucked in behind Grasmere Garden Centre, opposite the church. ☎ 015394 35245

Allan Bank
Prominent white house on high ground to north-west of village centre. Occupied by the Wordsworths from 1808 to 1811, although William had earlier expressed disapproval of its white colour and its impact on the landscape.
He planted some screening trees. Not open to the public.

Rowing Boats
Small boat hire premises a short distance along the road past the garden centre.

Grasmere Church, where Wordsworth lies buried

WALKS IN THE TROUTBECK, AMBLESIDE & GRASMERE AREA

1 Troutbeck village and church

A short, easy walk passing a wonderful array of traditional buildings and the parish church. 3.5km (2.25 miles).

Park in a small, informal parking area close to Church Bridge in the valley bottom. From Windermere turn left into a lane immediately after crossing the bridge and before reaching the church. The parking area is on the left. Walk up the lane to the road junction in the village. The former bank barn with the spinning gallery is on the left, before the stores.

At the road junction turn left to walk a short distance to Townend. Return to the junction and continue along the road, passing various connected hamlets, each with its fine old buildings. After passing the Mortal Man, turn right at a building with a clock on the wall and descend back towards the Mortal Man. This is High Green hamlet.

Keep to the left of the inn to follow a footpath which heads in a fairly straight lane towards the church. At the church join the main road, turning right to return to the parking area.

Great Rigg from Loughrigg Terrace

WALKS

2 ↑
•••

Wansfell Pike

484m (1,588 feet) Circular walk of 8km (5 miles) with a steep climb but no real difficulty underfoot. Ambleside's own mountain, with good views over the town and surrounding countryside.

Start up the road behind the Salutation, towards the waterfall, Stock Ghyll Force. After passing the fall, turn right at a junction of paths to head uphill towards the top of Wansfell Pike, visible ahead. The path is well used and has been much repaired to counter erosion. The way is never in doubt.

Continue over the top, along a path heading towards Troutbeck. Reach a cross wall in less than 1km (0.6 mile) and turn right on the far side. For about the same distance this path is a little vague but there is intermittent way marking. By an attractive little stream bear left to follow a rough roadway (Hundreds Road).

At a junction by the foot of this roadway, turn sharp right through a gate and descend to High Skelghyll Farm, continuing into Skelghyll Wood, where the celebrated Jenkin Crag viewpoint is passed. On reaching a major junction of paths, turn left, downhill to Waterhead or carry straight on to reach the main A591 road close to Hayes Garden Centre in Ambleside.

3 ↑
•••

Rydal Park and Under Loughrigg

A gentle stroll of 6km (3.75 miles) which can be enjoyed at all times, even without boots!

From Ambleside set off along the side of the main A591 Grasmere and Keswick road. Turn right at a gate which gives access to Rydal Park and follow the broad trackway across this attractive park land. At Rydal Hall, the right of way passes between the buildings, to the rear of the Hall itself. Short excursions to view the gardens and the waterfall may be possible. There is a teashop.

On reaching the cul-de-sac road close to Rydal Mount, turn left to descend to the main road. Turn left for a short distance, and then right to cross the River Rothay by a road bridge. Follow the minor Under Loughrigg road for nearly 2km (1.25 miles).

Turn left to cross the river by a bridge. There is now a junction of paths. Go ahead to return to Ambleside by the main car park, or turn to the right to cross another bridge and return by Rothay Park and the church.

4 ↑ *Loughrigg Terrace and the 'Coffin Road'*

●●●● A circuit of 8 km (5 miles) (shorter version available), which embraces all the best of Rydal and the Vale of Grasmere. A fair amount of comparatively gentle up and down, but no hills or mountains.

From the cul de sac road at Rydal, cross the main road, turning right for a short distance. Turn left to cross the River Rothay on a footbridge. Turn right after the bridge to follow a good path rising gently above Rydal Water.

After passing the far end of the lake there is a major junction of paths.

For the shorter version, turn right here, to descend through woodland to a bridge across the River Rothay. Cross the river and turn right to reach part of the White Moss car parking area, with public conveniences. Go up to the main road, cross, turn right for a few metres, and ascend a stony track to the left. At the top, join another track and turn right. This is the 'Coffin Road', clear on the ground all the way back to Rydal.

For the full circuit go straight on at the junction. This is now the famous Loughrigg Terrace, giving wonderful views over the Vale of Grasmere. At the far end of the Terrace a path to the left gives direct access to the summit of Loughrigg Fell (335m (1,099 feet).

Bend slightly right to go through woodland, angling towards the road which comes over Red Bank from Elterwater. Join the road and descend to Grasmere. Turn right by the church, walk to the main road, and take the minor road opposite. Pass Dove Cottage as this minor road climbs towards a tiny tarn. Leave the through road to keep uphill, then bend right by a seat. This is the 'Coffin Road' which loses its surface to become a rough trackway and then a bridleway as it keeps close under Nab Scar on its return to Rydal.

William

sk any visitor the name of a famous poet associated with the Lake District and, even from those who have never read a poem in their lives, there is only one possible answer – William Wordsworth.

YOUTH

Wordsworth was born in 1770 at Cockermouth. Of the four other Wordsworth children, William's sister Dorothy, 21 months his junior, was much the most significant. The family home in Cockermouth is a handsome Georgian house of modest size in the main street, now in the care of the National Trust.

Whilst living with relatives in Penrith, as small children William and Dorothy attended Mrs. Birkett's dame school, beside the churchyard; Mary (later to marry William) and Sara Hutchinson were fellow pupils. The building is still in existence as a coffee shop.

In 1778 his mother died and William's education continued at Hawkshead Grammar School where, with his brothers, he was a pupil from 1778-87. The school is open to visitors, its prime exhibit being the desk upon which Wordsworth carved his initials.

On leaving Cambridge William was something of a wanderer, without any clear idea of what he wanted to do in life and with quite radical political opinions.

During a second French visit in 1791–2, a love affair resulted in the birth of a daughter, Caroline. Although, mainly because of family and the long drawn out Napoleonic War between Britain and France, marriage was not possible, William always acknowledged his responsibility.

DOROTHY & MARRIAGE

On returning to Britain, William was reunited with his devoted sister Dorothy, beginning the lifelong relationship in which her role as his closest friend, soul mate and provider of much of his inspiration has constantly intrigued biographers and others.

After several years in the West Country, William and Dorothy returned to the Lake District for good in 1799, taking the tenancy of Dove Cottage, a small former inn at Town End, Grasmere. The first poems had been published in 1793 and in the now highly conducive surroundings William was soon in full spate, producing what is widely regarded as his finest work.

He married Mary Hutchinson in 1802, producing five children, whilst Dorothy remained as part of a happy triumvirate. Dove Cottage, largely in its original state, and the adjacent barn conversion to form the Wordsworth Museum, are administered by the Wordsworth Trust as a compelling visitor attraction.

Dove Cottage, Grasmere

Wordsworth

By 1808 the extended family had outgrown the cottage and moved to Allan Bank, a substantial house above Grasmere village.

From 1811–13 the Wordsworths lived in the Parsonage opposite Grasmere church. This turned out to be a most unhappy period as the house was dark and damp and two of their children – Thomas (6) and Catherine (4) – died. The final move of house was to Rydal Mount in 1813, living here until his death in 1850. The house is open to visitors.

As his fame spread, so William's youthful ardour mellowed and he became more of an establishment figure. The ultimate accolade was the award of the Poet Laureate title in 1843.

WITH THE LAKES POETS

Wordsworth's relationships over the years with other poets and writers – The Lakes Poets – are second in importance only to his relationship with Dorothy.

Having met and greatly admired Samuel Taylor Coleridge during his years in the West Country, the two were reunited in Lakeland in a brilliantly creative association. Coleridge's son Hartley was also associated with Wordsworth.

Another odd character was Thomas De Quincey, an opium addict who, after admiring Wordsworth from afar for many years eventually succeeded him as tenant of Dove Cottage.

Of all the 'Lakes Poets' the most enduring bond was that between Robert Southey and Wordsworth. Southey, with his large family, lived at Greta Hall Keswick for 40 years until his death in 1843. William often made the long walk from Grasmere or Rydal over to Keswick to visit his old friend.

Wordsworth's enduring fame is based firmly on his massive output of poetry such as the great autobiographical poem *The Prelude*, for enthusiasts, and shorter, more accessible, pieces such as *The Daffodils* (by the Ullswater shore at Gowbarrow Park) and *The Rainbow* for a wider audience.

GUIDE TO THE LAKES

In his own lifetime, his prose work *Guide to the Lakes* was far more successful than any of the published poetry.

The fifth edition of 1845, as republished with an introduction and notes by Ernest de Selincourt, is still available.

Two themes emerge strongly from the guide. First, that by today's standards Wordsworth was highly opinionated and had what we would call a snobbish view of the lack of ability of the lower orders of society to appreciate the beauty of the finer things of life such as Lakeland scenery. Second, and more to his credit, he emerges as a true, probably the first, Lake District environmentalist, at that early stage recognising the fragility of the local landscape and almost uncannily foreseeing the adverse effects which unsuitable development could have on that landscape.

Together with several members of his family, Wordsworth lies at the far end of the churchyard in Grasmere, where the soothing murmur of the waters of the River Rothay would have pleased him greatly.

Beatrix Potter

*P*eter Rabbit is undoubtedly one of the most famous characters in children's literature, along with favourites such as Jeremy Fisher, Jemima Puddleduck and Tom Kitten. All these are, of course, animals given human characteristics by their creator, Beatrix Potter, who wrote the stories, and drew and painted the illustrations.

Contrary to popular belief, Beatrix Potter was not born in the Lake District but in London, in the year 1866. Typical of the Victorian era, she was educated at home by a series of nannies and governesses. She was 16 years of age when she first visited the Lake District; her parents had rented **Wray Castle** near Ambleside for their annual holiday.

SAWREY

A few years passed before the Potter parents took over **Larkfield** (now **Eeswyke Country House Hotel**) for another of their long sojourns. Beatrix loved this house with its fine views of Esthwaite Water. She described Sawrey 'as near perfect a little place as I have ever lived in'. It was then, at the age of 30, that she decided that somehow, sometime, a small part of this area would belong to her.

In 1905 she purchased, mainly from the royalties earned from her books for children, **Hill Top Farm** in Sawrey. Whilst living at Hill Top she wrote more of the little books, finding inspiration in the animals, buildings, and countryside of Sawrey and Hawkshead. In *The P ie and the P atty -pan* the cat Ribby and the small dog Duchess were owned by people in Sawrey, the story being set in cottages in the village. The tales of Tom Kitten, Jemima Puddleduck, and Tabitha Twitchet, are similarly set in Sawrey, Hawkshead, and the lakes, fields and lanes within a few miles of Hill Top Farm.

MARRIAGE

Increasing popularity and sales of the books enabled Beatrix to acquire more farms and land. Through these negotiations she met **William Heelis**, a local solicitor. From a business-based relationship a friendship developed; William married Beatrix in 1913. She was then 47 and William was about two years her junior. The couple started their married life in another

Hill Top, Sawrey

and the National Trust

property owned by Beatrix in Sawrey. William would ride his motorbike to and from his office in Hawkshead. (The building is now **The Beatrix Potter Gallery** owned by the National Trust and open to the public. See chapter 4).

For Beatrix, life changed considerably following her marriage; she now lived permanently in the Lake District. Writing books became less important to her – perhaps because she was now surrounded by live animals she felt less need to fantasise about them. However, farming, rural life, and land management became more time absorbing and demanding.

THE NATIONAL TRUST

Some years before her marriage Beatrix had been introduced by her father to **Canon Hardwick Rawnsley**, one of the three eminent people who founded the National Trust. Beatrix shared the Canon's ideals for preservation and conservation of the countryside. The friendship between Canon Rawnsley and Beatrix continued until his death shortly after the end of the First World War. His opinions were to bear on Beatrix for the remainder of her life and to have far-reaching influence in perpetuity.

Mrs Heelis was a shrewd businesswoman. With her husband's undoubted local knowledge and assistance, she purchased property and land in the locality; this helped to ensure that farms and estates were not broken down into units too small to remain viable. At the time of her death in 1943 she owned over 4,000 acres of land, 15 farms, large flocks of Herdwick sheep (a very hardy local breed) and numerous houses and cottages. This vast estate was given to the National Trust, the bequest showing the esteem and faith that Beatrix had in the ability of this relatively new organisation to protect and conserve vulnerable parts of the Lake District.

Many visitors ask where to find the grave of Beatrix Potter – it does not exist. She was cremated, her ashes scattered in an unknown place by Tom Storey, her faithful servant and farm manager at Hill Top.

IN HER FOOTSTEPS

This very brief biography of Beatrix Potter may tempt the visitor to explore the settings for her books and the land and farms she owned – but do remember that many are private residences – and the lovely villages of Sawrey and Hawkshead. Hill Top Farm is a justifiably popular place to visit (owned by the National Trust). At the Beatrix Potter Gallery in Hawkshead there is an exhibition of the original drawings and paintings. The display changes each year. Part of the building is furnished as it was when used as the busy office of William Heelis and Co., Solicitors.

4

Langdale, Coniston & Hawkshead

• LANGDALE •

Easily reached from the M6 motorway and the railway station at Windermere, for the great majority of visitors Great Langdale provides the readiest access to the heart of Lake District mountain country.

The head of the valley is dominated by the great bulk of the Crinkle Crags and Bowfell, while the ice-scraped sides embrace a fine example of a textbook U-shaped valley. Most characteristic, and visible from far away on the approach to Lakeland, are the **Langdale Pikes**, by no means the highest of the mountains but unmistakable in their uncompromisingly rocky outline. Rock climbers have long practised their skills on buttresses such as Gimmer Crag.

The lower reaches of the valley are altogether more gentle, with woodland and the rather elusive small lake of Elterwater. Below Skelwith Bridge the Great Langdale Beck becomes the River Brathay for its short remaining journey to the head of Windermere.

The whole of this area is prime walking country, ranging from a gentle stroll between Skelwith Bridge and Elterwater village to the hard day's march to Scafell Pikes and back.

The two villages in Great Langdale are **Elterwater** and **Chapel Stile**. Elterwater sits attractively at the foot of a great common, surely on a fine day one of the best picnic sites imaginable, with the immensely popular Brittania Inn providing snug comfort in less clement weather. South of the village an immense quarry provides the fine, highly esteemed, green Lakeland slate.

Gig House Gallery

Elterwater. Original paintings by artists in all media, both local and from further afield.

Holy Trinity Church

Brathay. Italianate structure of 1836 on an open site above the River Brathay, a little way beyond Clappersgate. Fine wood carving and brass memorials inside.

Chapel Stile is also well situated below the wide bulk of Silver Howe, with the solidly built parish church prominent. By the side of the main road, a little way short of the village, is Landdales Hotel, a hotel and bar managed by the Langdale timeshare group.

Skelwith Bridge is merely a hamlet at an important road junction, with hotel and bar and the Kirkstone Gallery. Each village has a general store.

Kirkstone Gallery

Skelwith Bridge. Extensive gallery/shop, with Lake District slate for sale, both natural and manufactured into a variety of fireplaces, ornaments, etc. Good teashop with light meals.
☎ 015394 34002

Holy Trinity Church

Chapel Stile. On the site of an earlier chapel, this sturdy, no-nonsense, structure is of the mid 19th century. Inside there is good wood carving and a window with brightly coloured glass in the south wall. Before 1821 burials were not allowed here and the coffins had to be carried up the valley side and over the top to Grasmere.

Right: Blea Tarn House offers Bed & Breakfast in stunning scenery

Opposite page: The Three Shires in Little Langdale

Car parks are to be found:

(1) in a former quarry on the right, a little way past Skelwith Bridge

(2) opposite the Brittania Inn, Elterwater village

(3) on the lower part of Elterwater Common

(4) opposite the New Dungeon Ghyll Hotel

(5) on the right just beyond the New Dungeon Ghyll Hotel

(6) at the Old Dungeon Ghyll Hotel.

Dungeon Ghyll, from which the two hotels derive their names, is a ravine descending precipitously from the Langdale Pikes behind the New Dungeon Ghyll Hotel. There are three waterfalls in the ravine, of which the lowest may be safely visited by those prepared to climb up the path from the hotel. The two upper falls form part of a sporting route to the top of Harrison Stickle or Pike of Stickle.

As the valley road in Great Langdale seems to be heading for a dead end by the Old Dungeon Ghyll, a sudden left twist takes it past Wall End Farm and then steeply (25 per cent) uphill to Blea Tarn, where there is another car park and wonderful views back to the Langdale Pikes.

The subsequent descent is into **Little Langdale**, another fine valley, less dramatic than its bigger neighbour but with its own little tarn and with mountains such as Wetherlam, Pike of Blisco and the Crinkle Crags all close in view. From the junction at the foot of the hill, the road to the right

New Dungeon Ghyll Hotel, Old Dungeon Ghyll Hotel

Two old, traditional, hostelries, which have long been landmarks in Great Langdale and the starting points for important walkers' routes. Now serving a wide variety of food and drink to suit all tastes.

climbs over one of the great passes, Wrynose, to the Duddon valley. The beck from Little Langdale Tarn tumbles down Colwith Force (waterfall) on its way to Elterwater. The valley has no villages but the Three Shires Inn, with a hamlet including a part-time post office, is a focal point.

• CONISTON •

Beautifully situated between mountains and lake, the former mining and quarrying village of Coniston has transformed itself into a popular destination for visitors, full of bustling activity at most times of year. Shops and inns, such as the 16th-century Black Bull, patronised by Coleridge and De Quincey, offer plenty of choice in the compact village centre.

Best known of the shapely group of mountains over-looking Coniston is Coniston Old Man, most southerly of the great Lakeland peaks and a particular favourite locally.

Copper Mines Valley

1.5km (1 mile) above Coniston. Heart of the formerly great mining industry with remains and shafts, scattered over a wide area. Attempts are being made to provide limited visitor facilities, including museum and interpretation displays.

Below: Coniston Village

Opposite: The Coniston launch at Brantwood

Coniston Water is very attractive; several of the locations used by Arthur Ransome in his *Swallows and Amazons* children's stories are based on actual places on and around this lake and Windermere. In the 1950s and 60s it became well known nationally and internationally when the Campbells, Sir Malcolm and Donald, father and son, made several attempts, successful and otherwise, on the world water speed record here. The attempts ended in tragedy in 1967 when *Bluebird* somersaulted at about 483km (300 miles) per hour. Donald's body has never been found. There is a simple memorial at the junction of Tilberthwaite Avenue and Ruskin Avenue.

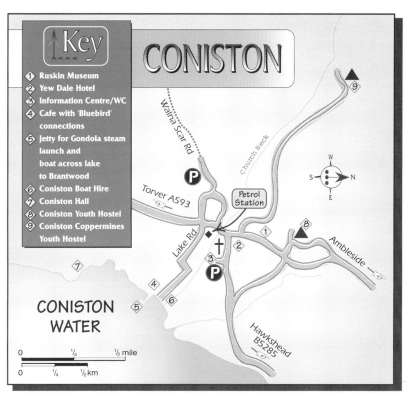

CONISTON

Key

1. Ruskin Museum
2. Yew Dale Hotel
3. Information Centre/WC
4. Cafe with 'Bluebird' connections
5. Jetty for Gondola steam launch and boat across lake to Brantwood
6. Coniston Boat Hire
7. Coniston Hall
8. Coniston Youth Hostel
9. Coniston Coppermines Youth Hostel

Walna Scar Rd

Church Beck

Torver A593

Lake Rd

Petrol Station

Ambleside

Hawkshead B5285

CONISTON WATER

0   ¼   ½ mile
0   ¼   ½ km

Gondola

A beautiful steam launch of 1859, abandoned and derelict for many years. Restored and operated by the National Trust. Operates to a scheduled daily timetable from late March to the end of October, weather permitting. Sailings from the Coniston jetty, at the end of the cul-de-sac Lake Road (less than 1 km – 0.6 mile) start at 11.00, except on Saturdays, when commencement is about an hour later. Calling points at Brantwood and at Park-a-Moor at the south-east end of the lake.
☎ 015394 63849

Across the lake the impressive house with the fine situation overlooking both lake and mountains is **Brantwood,** home of John Ruskin, philosopher, poet, painter and social reformer, from 1872 until his death in 1900. In many ways, Ruskin was to Coniston what Wordsworth was to Grasmere and Rydal.

A foot ferry service links Brantwood to Coniston during the season, with limited Sunday sailings in winter. Ruskin's grave is at the back of the churchyard in the middle of Coniston; the memorial is of local stone, carved to designs by the celebrated local historian W.G. Collingwood, for many years Ruskin's secretary. The designs depict Ruskin's principal interests – The Guild of St George craft organisation, poetry, music, nature, science and some of his principal writings such as *The Stones of Venice* and *Seven Lamps of Architecture*.

Brantwood

Elegant 18th-century house purchased, extended and renovated by John Ruskin. Became one of the greatest literary and artistic centres in Europe. Displays of Ruskin's drawings and watercolours; video programme; bookshop; special exhibitions; tearoom with light meals; nature trails; lake shore and woodland gardens. Open to visitors daily mid March to mid November 11.00–17.30; Wednesday to Sunday 11.00–16.00 in winter. Closed Christmas Day and Boxing Day. ☎ 015394 41396

The main car park, with Tourist Information Office and public conveniences is close to the centre, accessed from Tilberthwaite Avenue. A smaller car park is on the site of the former railway station, steeply uphill along Station Road. There is also car parking by the lake shore.

MORE PLACES TO VISIT
• Coniston •

Coniston Old Hall
1.5km (1 mile) from the village centre, close to the lake shore. The oldest surviving building in the area, claimed to be based on an ancient defensive pele tower. Now used for farming and as reception for a camping site. Not open to the public but a right of way passes close by.

St Andrew's Parish Church
On the site of an older chapel, the present building is of the 19th century, including a general renovation in 1891. Ruskin memorial in graveyard.

Lake Ferry
The *Coniston Launch*, accommodating more than 50 passengers, plies between Coniston, Monk Coniston (Waterhead), Brantwood and Torver several times a day in season – late March to the end of October. Limited sailings on some winter Sundays. A very useful link to Brantwood, with a small discount on combined ticket. Also special interest cruises in high season.
Free car parking at Waterhead.
☎/fax 015394 36216

Coniston Boating Centre
Sheltered bay with gravel beach close to the Coniston jetty (see above). Operated by the National Park Authority. Electric launches, rowing boats, sailing dinghies and Canadian canoes for hire. Firm slipway, car parking, picnic area and café. ☎ 015394 41366

Brantwood, the home of John Ruskin

Museum
Small museum in Yewdale Road, renovated 1997-99. Specialises in Ruskin memorabilia. ☎ Tourist Information Office.

Summitreks Ltd
14, Yewdale Road, Coniston Adventure activities on lake and mountains. Equipment for hire. ☎ 015394 41212

Tourist Information Office
By the main car park.
☎ 015394 41533

• HAWKSHEAD •

East of Coniston is the popular village of Hawkshead. Once a remote, off the beaten track, self-sufficient little market town, set in the gentle countryside of south Lakeland, Hawkshead is now readily accessible to visitors and has become a very popular place indeed. With white-painted buildings, many of considerable antiquity, clustered around small squares and narrow alleyways, it is quite unlike any other Lake District town or village.

Hawkshead Grammar School

Across the village street from the car park. Founded in 1585 by locally born Edward Sandys who became Archbishop of York.
The present building dates from 1675 and the school continued in use until 1909. William Wordsworth was a pupil here from 1779 to 1787. A desk on which he carved his initials can still be seen. Upstairs is a famous old bible and initials carved on a windowsill by Wordsworth's brother John.
Open to the public Easter to October, daily 10.00–12.30, 13.30–17.00; Sundays 13.00–17.00. Closes 16.30 in October.
Admission charge.

Partial pedestrianisation has been a great advantage, making Hawkshead one of the best places to wander on foot. The mixture of shops, including a National Trust shop, caters well for both residents and visitors, whilst four inns, tea and coffee shops all compete to provide varied refreshments. The associations with William Wordsworth and Beatrix Potter add considerably to visitor interest.

The former office of Beatrix's solicitor husband, William Heelis, is now open as the **Beatrix Potter Gallery** displaying a selection of the 500 or so watercolours and drawings which provided the wonderful illustrations for the famous books. The selection on display is changed each year; enthusiasts will be able to recognise some of the buildings of Hawkshead and district which provide the background to the characters in the books.

Car parking is close to the village centre, approached from the main road which bypasses the village.

North of the village centre, 0.6km (0.3 mile) along the B5286 towards Ambleside, stands the **Old Courthouse,** a gatehouse which is the only surviving portion of the former Hawkshead Hall. Formerly used by the monks of Furness Abbey as an outpost from which they administered the estates in this

Above: Balloon flights from Hawkshead give superb views of the area

Below: Hawkshead Court House, now owned by the National Trust

area, it was later used as a courthouse, hence the name. There is nothing to see inside but the key is available from either the National Trust shop or the Beatrix Potter Gallery in Hawkshead.

MORE PLACES TO VISIT
• Hawkshead•

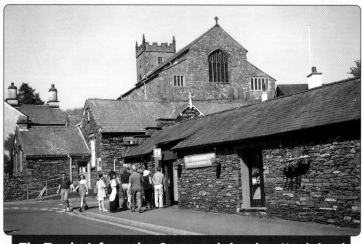

The Tourist Information Centre and church at Hawkshead

St Michael and All Angels Church

Part of the structure, including the tower, is more than 700 years old, side aisles being added in about 1500. Wordsworth's 'snow white church upon her hill'. The white-painted rough cast was removed in 1875/76. Sandys family private chapel. Primitive dug-out chest about 400 years old. Season of summer evening concerts.

Ann Tyson's Cottage

Reached through a narrow passage by the Methodist church. Boys from the Grammar School, including William Wordsworth, lodged here with Ann Tyson for some years. Not open to the public.

Red Lion Inn, Main Street

Claimed to be a 15th-century coaching Inn. Two interesting carved figures high on the front wall, one depicting a farmer taking his pig to market and the other of a man holding the whistle which was blown at market opening time.

Trout Fishing, Esthwaite Water

The Boathouse, on the west side of the lake. Brown and rainbow trout may be fished from hire boats and from the shoreline. Rods available for hire. Fly-fishing tuition can be given (minimum two days' notice). ☎ 015394 36541

Tourist Information Centre

Main car park.
☎ 015394 36525

• GRIZEDALE & THE FAR SOUTH •

A substantial area of land to the south of Hawkshead, between Coniston Water and Windermere has long been covered by the commercial forestry of the former Forestry Commission, now Forest Enterprises. This is Grizedale where in recent years there has been a more enlightened and visitor friendly approach to the operation of these vast woodlands than was previously the case. More regard is paid to the conservation of natural life and the environment generally; planting in this area is quite diverse in species and there are substantial clear areas.

A particular feature of this forest is that visitors are positively encouraged by the provision of a comprehensive **visitor centre**, the creation of numerous trails for walkers and cyclists and, by no means least, a great number of diverse and ingenious **sculptures in wood** along most of the trails, adding interest and a touch of whimsicality.

Grizedale Visitor Centre

Forestry interpretation exhibits of many kinds. Shop. Tearoom, with light meals available. Art/craft gallery. Children's play area. Cycle hire. Theatre in the Forest – plays, talks and musical concerts. Car parks at the centre and further afield for walks or rides on the forest trails. Trail maps available at visitor centre. Forest trails of varying length as indicated by the map at the visitor centre. One of the best walks is along the designated Silurian Way, which has about 80 of the famous sculptures.
☎ 01229 860010

Near Sawrey is an attractive village along the B5285 road from Hawkshead to the Windermere ferry, close to Esthwaite Water. The prime attraction is Beatrix Potter's house, **Hill Top**, which has became a mecca for Beatrix Potter enthusiasts from all over the world. Many of the scenes which provide the background to the characters in the illustrations of the famous children's books can be found in and around Near Sawrey.

Hill Top was purchased by Beatrix Potter with the earnings from her first book, *The Tale of Peter Rabbit*, and a small legacy. For some years she spent as much time as she could at Hill Top, furnishing it very much to her own taste. During this time she wrote the other children's books. After her marriage in 1913 she moved to nearby Castle Cottage, not open to the public, keeping Hill Top as a studio, study and private place of relaxation.

Hill Top

Beatrix Potter's home, kept almost exactly as it was in her day, complete with her furniture and china. Open to the public late March–end of October, Saturdays–Wednesdays and Good Friday, 11.00–17.00. Admission by timed ticket. Shop open every day 10.00–17.00. Admission charge.
☎ 015394 36269

Also of interest is the Tower Bank Arms, with its clock, a traditional village inn which is in National Trust ownership, a very rare situation indeed. The National Trust car park is not very easy to find. From the Windermere approach it is about 100m past the Tower Bank Arms, on the left.

Further along the road towards the Windermere ferry lies **Far Sawrey**, another quite substantial village with a hotel, general store and the parish church.

Left & below: These cottages and the Tower Bank Arms feature in Beatrix Potter's books. Her house is behind the Tower Bank Arms.

• THE RUSLAND VALLEY, NEWBY BRIDGE, LAKESIDE, AND HAVERTHWAITE •

In this area there are no towns or large villages, no mountains and no lake other than the southern tip of Windermere so, not surprisingly, this is one of the less busy parts of the district. In spite of that, there is a great deal here for visitors, and the comparatively gentle, quiet, countryside is unfailingly attractive.

The Lakeside to Haverthwaite Steam Railway

The **Rusland Valley** is a charming backwater served only by minor roads. From Grizedale head south through Satterthwaite and the tiny former industrial settlements of Force Mills and Force Forge. Even more minor is the direct road from Hawkshead, via the western shore of Esthwaite Water. From the south the road is from Haverthwaite, through Bouth. Rusland church has a commanding position in the valley with lovely views from the churchyard, which is the resting place of the children's author Arthur Ransome.

A short distance below the outfall from Windermere is **Newby Bridge, a** large, impressive, stone-arched structure across the River Leven. A small settlement has grown around this important river crossing, including two sizeable hotels. Downstream of the bridge is the weir which regulates the water level in Windermere.

At the foot of Windermere, on the west side lies the hamlet of **Lakeside,** the southern terminus of the scheduled 'steamer' service on the lake and the northern terminus of the **Lakeside and Haverthwaite railway** line. Interchange facility and combined tickets are available. The railway is a branch line of the former Furness Railway, which left the main line near Ulverston and terminated at Lakeside, being closed by British Railways in 1967. The length from Haverthwaite to Lakeside has subsequently been taken over by a preservation group and reopened as a visitor attraction, using steam locomotives for haulage.

Lakeside & Haverthwaite Railway

Depot with static railway exhibits and visitor facilities including car parking, shop, café, toilets, at Haverthwaite, 4km (2.5 miles) southwest of Newby Bridge on the A590 main road. Steam-hauled trains operate during the Easter period, weekends in April, and daily from early May to the end of October.
☎ 015395 31594

Stott Park Bobbin Mill

Minimal restoration has been carried out by English Heritage and the mill is now a wonderful working museum with 19th-century machinery, powered by the steam engine on Tuesdays, Wednesdays and Thursdays and electrically on other days. Admission charge. Wheelchair access to ground floor. Toilets. Car park.
Open late March to the end of October, daily 10.00–18.00 (last tour 17.00). ☎ 015395 31087

On the road to Hawkshead, 1km (0.6 mile) north of Lakeside is the **Stott Park Bobbin Mill.** Built in 1835, this was one of a large number of similar mills which combined the coppiced woodland and abundant water power of south Lakeland to produce vast quantities of wooden bobbins for the Lancashire cotton industry. The mill also used its lathes to make a variety of other wooden articles.

The introduction of plastic bobbins and the shrinkage of the cotton trade rapidly killed off the bobbin mills. Stott Park was one of the last to close, in 1971. The machinery was originally powered by a waterwheel, later a combination of water turbine and steam engine, and latterly by electricity.

MORE PLACES TO VISIT NEAR
• Newby Bridge •

Fell Foot Country Park
7 hectares (17 acres) of gardens and park at the foot of Windermere, accessed from the A592 Newby Bridge to Bowness road. Owned by the National Trust. Formerly the garden of a grand house, long demolished, Fell Foot now offers car parks, formal garden, children's adventure playground, picnic areas, informal lake swimming – with care! – rowing-boat hire, slipway, toilets, shop and tearoom serving light lunches. There is a passenger ferry across the lake to Lakeside (see below). Occasional theatre productions. Charge per car. Open all year daily, park and garden: 09.00–19.00 (or dusk if earlier). Shop and tearoom - late March–end October, 11.00–17.00. ☎ 015395 31273

The Aquarium of the Lakes
Lakeside. Opened in 1997, this major attraction displays the water, animal, bird and plant life of a typical Lakeland river from mountain top to the final outfall into Morecambe Bay. Multimedia presentation. Water laboratory. 'Underwater' walk. Shop. Restaurant/café. Wheelchair access to all areas. Admission charge. Open daily from 09.00 throughout year except Christmas Day. ☎ 015395 30153

Stott Park Bobbin Mill, near Lakeside

Artcrystal
Clock Tower Buildings, Low Wood, Haverthwaite. Crystal glass engraving studio. Visitors welcome. Shop. Free admission. ☎ 015395 31796

Abbots Reading Farm Museum and Rare Breeds Centre
Haverthwaite. Accessed from the main A590, Newby Bridge to Barrow road, turning north at Haverthwaite cross roads (signpost – Grizedale Forest), then right at Causeway End. 1km (0.6 mile) from the main road. Rare breeds of farm animals. Collection of agricultural machinery and bygones. Picnic area and children's play area.

WALKS

1 ↑ Scafell Pikes

At 978m (3,210 feet), the highest mountain in England, Scafell Pikes has an obvious attraction for those with the necessary strength and determination. Often climbed from Great Langdale by a quite long – 17.5km (11 miles) – return walk. No particular difficulty, but the ability to walk safely on rough rocks of all shapes and sizes is required.

Set off from the Old Dungeon Ghyll Hotel along the broad track up Mickleden, now part of the Cumbria Way. At a junction of paths by a footbridge keep left and tackle the prolonged and rugged ascent of Rosset Gill. There are path variations here, but all emerge at the same place at the top, just above Angle Tarn.

Drop a little, pass the tarn, and climb again, with Great End impressive ahead. Turn left at a cross paths and rise to Esk Hause, another junction of routes. Turn right here to climb up Calf Cove and gain the Scafell Pikes summit ridge, a broad, stony wilderness. Bear left along the ridge, passing Broad Crag on the way to the summit.

After due admiration of the extensive view, the easiest return by far is by retracing the outward route.

Elterwater from the lakeside path

Skelwith Bridge and Elterwater

2

A truly gentle valley bottom ramble of 2.5km (1.5 miles), with a waterfall and Elterwater as prime attractions. This route offers the only opportunity of being close to the lake. The views up the valley, dominated by the Langdale Pikes, are superb.

Parking at Skelwith Bridge is limited; a disused quarry on the right a little further along the Langdale road provides a good alternative. If this car park is used, cross the road to find the path to Elterwater, which is joined after Skelwith Force. A left turn is then needed to view the waterfall.

From Skelwith Bridge take the path beside the Kirkstone Galleries and through the slate dressing works behind the galleries. Sandwiched between the River Brathay and the road, the path soon reaches the famous waterfall, not high, but with impressively surging power. Keep hold of small children!

Continue along the unmistakable path, across fields and through the bog woodland by the side of the lake, all too soon reaching Elterwater village opposite the Brittania Inn. To return, retrace the route or catch the bus.

With time and energy to spare continue along the valley; for the most part the road can be avoided.

From Elterwater village, use the quarry approach road to access a signposted footpath reaching the road by the Langdales Hotel, then another road-avoiding path for a short distance, then along the road before reaching the near end of the former valley road. This road was replaced by the present road due to persistent flooding and now makes a good route for walkers as far as the New Dungeon Ghyll Hotel.

From the back of the hotel a rougher but still acceptable path stays parallel with the road all the way to the Old Dungeon Ghyll Hotel, terminus of the valley bus service.

From Elterwater village to the Old Dungeon Ghyll Hotel is a very level walk of 8km (5 miles).

WALKS

3↑ Coniston Old Man
●●●●

At 803m (2,635 feet), the highest point of the Coniston group of fells, the Old Man is the obvious first choice for a mountain walk. There are several routes from the Coniston area to the top, but the one below is the most straightforward. An out and back ascent is a total of 9km (5.5 miles); the full recommended circuit is 13km (8 miles). There are no difficulties involved.

Go past the Sun Inn and through Dixon Ground Farm, soon rising by the side of the turbulent Church Beck. Don't cross Miners' Bridge with its waterfall, but keep left to ascend the hillside by a well-marked path.

The route goes through extensive old quarry workings before reaching Levers Water. From here the ascent is steep, with twists and turns before reaching the fine summit. On a clear day the extensive views include the Isle of Man.

Return routes are many and varied as more of the adjacent peaks can readily be included in a day's walk. The broad ridges of this group of fells are exceptionally kind underfoot. A good circuit is as follows:

Head north from the Old Man, dropping to Levers Hause before rising again to Swirl How (801m – 2,630 feet). A right turn here gives a descent along the Prison Band ridge, with a final rise to Wetherlam (762m – 2,501feet). From this last peak there are two footpaths to the right, both heading roughly south towards Coniston. The more westerly path drops quickly into the Red Dell valley, whilst the well-used, more easterly path keeps its height for some distance along the broad south ridge of Wetherlam.

Either will complete an excellent mountain circuit.

4↑ Tarn Hows
●●●●

3km (2 miles). One of Lakeland's finest jewels, a beautiful little lake in a partially wooded setting, with the Coniston fells providing the perfect backdrop. There is a National Trust car park adjacent to the tarn, reached from Coniston by the B5285 Hawkshead road making two left turns in the Hawkshead Hill area (signposted). From Hawkshead, turn right at Hawkshead Hill. A limited access for wheelchair users has been created by the Trust.

Tarn Hows, arguably the most attractive and most photographed place in the Lakes

Walk down from the car park and continue around the tarn in either a clockwise or anti-clockwise direction; either is delightful and needs no route guidance.

5 ↑ *Gummers How*

Only 321m (1,054 feet) in height, but a fine viewpoint at the south end of Windermere. Easily climbed from a nearby car park by a short walk of 2km (1.3 miles) there and back. Total ascent about 110m (361 feet).

Opposite Fell Foot Country Park leave the A592 to take a minor road rising steeply towards Bowland Bridge in the Winster valley. Near the summit of the road there is a car park on the right.

Cross the road and take the obvious footpath which heads straight to the summit of the shapely little peak. Return by the same route.

CAR TOURS

The four itineraries set out below offer attractions of great diversity, in sufficient quantity to provide many happy days for the visitor. All are naturally much enhanced by the attractive countryside, ranging from the sandy estuary of the River Kent to the high, wind-swept, moorland above the Lune Valley.

1 Kendal – Sedbergh – Kirby Lonsdale – Kendal

From Kendal take the A684, heading east to Sedbergh, a fine little market town (Wednesday) just inside the boundary of the Yorkshire Dales National Park. Historic main street; cannons left by Bonnie Prince Charlie in 1745; well-known public school.

 Tourist Information Office ☎ 015396 20125

From Sedbergh head south along the Lune Valley, A683, to **Kirkby Lonsdale**, another historic market town (Thursday). It has a good square, old inns and narrow lanes with intriguing names. Don't miss **'Ruskin's View'** behind the churchyard, a fine panorama of the Lune Valley and Pennine Hills. St. Andrew's Church has a Norman base to the tower, with well-carved doorway. **Devil's Bridge** is a few minutes' walk to the south of the town, a high stone bridge over the river, with rocky scenery around, painted by J.M.W. Turner.

 Tourist Information Office ☎ 015242 71437

Leave Kirkby Lonsdale along the main road back to Kendal, A65, joining the A591 near Levens. To the left about 1km (0.6 mile) after the junction is **Sizergh Castle**, home of the Strickland family for more than 750 years and now in the care of the National Trust. Not uncommonly in this area the house is founded on a defensive pele tower which was extended in Tudor times. English and French furniture. Limestone rock garden.

Return to Kendal by A591/A6.

INCLUDING ADDITIONAL ATTRACTIONS

Sizergh Castle

House, gardens and tearoom. Most of garden, lower hall and tearoom accessible to wheelchair users. Wheelchair and powered mobility vehicle available. Admission charge. Car park. Open late March to end of October, Sunday–Thursday, 13.30–17.30 (last admission 17.00) Shop and garden are open on the same days from 12.30–17.30. Admission to garden only, at reduced charge. ☎ 015395 60070

CAR TOURS

2 ↑ Kendal – Levens Bridge – Beetham – Arnside – Kendal

●●●● Take the A6 to the south from Kendal, then A591, A590, A6. to Levens Bridge. From Windermere/Bowness take the A5074 Lyth Valley road and turn left on to A590, then right to A6. On the right is the entrance to Levens Hall, an Elizabethan mansion built around yet another 13th-century pele tower. The hall is the home of the Bagot family. Jacobean furniture, paintings, early English patchwork. The splendid gardens are particularly noted for the intricate topiary.

Levens Hall

Collection of working steam engines, operational 14.00–17.00. Wheelchair access to all areas except the house. Café serving lunches and teas; gift shop; plant centre; children's play area. Admission charge. House open 12.00–16.30 (last admission) Monday to Thursday from end of March to end of September. Gardens also open Sundays and Monday to Friday during October.

Continue along the A6, through Milnthorpe, to Beetham for the **Heron Corn Mill and Museum of Paper Making.** On the banks of the River Bela, this is one of the few working mills in the area, having been restored in 1975. Powered by a 4m (14ft) waterwheel, traditional machinery is still in place. In 1988 a barn on the site was refurbished to house the Museum of Paper Making.

Heron Corn Mill and Museum of Paper Making

Entered via Mill Lane, a sharp turn off A6. Admission charge. Open 11.00–17.00 daily except Mondays, from Easter (or 1 April if before Easter) until 30 September. Open Bank Holiday Mondays. ☎ 015395 63363; fax 015395 63869

From Beetham a minor road leads through Storth to **Arnside**, a pleasant village on the south side of the Kent estuary. The railway viaduct was finished, after a great deal of difficulty, by the engineer Brunlees in 1857. Turn left in Arnside and drive between Arnside Knott and Arnside Tower on its hill, to **Silverdale**. Along a minor road to the south of the village is **Wolf House Gallery,** housed in restored farm buildings. Here traditional and contemporary British crafts and paintings are displayed and may be purchased.

Wolf House Gallery

Adventure play area; tearoom. Open daily except Mondays from 1 April–24 December, 10.30–13.00 and 14.00–17.30. From January to Easter open Saturdays and Sundays only, 10.30–17.30. Closed Christmas Day and Boxing Day. ☎ 01524 701405

From Silverdale head east, over the railway, towards Yealand Conyers. Just after Silverdale station is the entrance to **Leighton Moss Nature Reserve**, a large and important reserve of the Royal Society for the Protection of Birds with a wonderful variety of waterfowl and other birds. Also deer, otters and at least 532 species of plants.

Leighton Moss Nature Reserve

Wheelchair access to several hides. Visitor centre and tearoom. No dogs allowed on the reserve. Open all year 09.00–21.00 (or sunset, if earlier). ☎ 01524 701601

Continue through Yealand Redmayne to Yealand Conyers and the entrance drive to **Leighton Hall**, a fine house built in grey limestone, with 19th-century garden and woodland walks in the extensive grounds. Very much a 'lived-in' house. Programme of special events each year, including antiques fairs, concert and fireworks and Shakespeare in the garden.

CAR TOURS

Leighton Hall

Collection of birds of prey. Tearooms. Admission charge. Open daily May to September, 14.00–17.00 (11.00–17.00 in August). Closed Saturdays and Mondays, except Bank Holiday Mondays.
☎ 01524 734474; fax 01524 720357

From Leighton Hall return to Yealand Conyers and turn right. Go through Warton and on to Carnforth. On entering the town look out for **Steamtown** signs before the railway station. Steamtown comprises a large collection of steam locomotives and other rolling stock on the site of the former locomotive depot and yard, with a short length of operating track.

Steamtown

Visitor facilities including tearoom, shop and toilets.
☎ 01524 732100

Cartmel with the abbey in the background

INCLUDING
ADDITIONAL ATTRACTIONS

Head up the A6 back towards Kendal. A short diversion at the second roundabout (2.5 km – 1.5 miles) towards Burton in Kendal reaches Tewitfield, just after the bridge over M6, on the long disused **Lancaster Canal**. For a few years this canal, one of the most scenic in the country, provided an important link between Kendal, Lancaster and Preston, with a branch to the sea at Glasson Dock. The arrival of the railway killed off the trade but the canal lingered on. Construction of the M6 motorway severed the waterway in several places but some lengths still have water navigable by shallow draft boats. At Tewitfield there is a small flight of locks.

Return to the A6 and turn right. In 6km (3.75 miles) on the left is the **Lakeland Wildlife Oasis**, half zoo and half museum with interactive hands-on exhibits and exotic wildlife, including butterfly house and tropical halls.

Lakeland Wildlife Oasis

Coffee/snack bar; gift shop; picnic facilities. Wheelchair access throughout. Admission charge. Car park. Open daily, except Christmas, from 10.00–18.00 (last admission 17.00) in summer 10.00–17.00 (last admission 16.00) in winter. ☎ 015395 63027

3 ↑ *Grange-over-Sands – Humphrey Head – Cartmel*

●●●● From Kendal take A6, A591/A590. From Windermere, Bowness, Ambleside and places north take A592 (Newby Bridge)/A590. From Coniston take A593/A5084/A5092/A590. In each case drive to Grange-over-Sands, a dignified little Victorian seaside town on the shore of Morecambe Bay, with tastefully laid out gardens and arcaded shops.

Continue along B5277 to Kent's Bank, one end of the famous route, still a public right of way, which crosses Morecambe Bay from Hest's Bank near Morecambe. Once crossed by coaches, this potentially hazardous route

CAR TOURS

should never be attempted without the assistance of the Queen's Guide.

Next is **Flookborough,** once a town with an ancient market charter but now comparatively sleepy, although still with some Morecambe Bay fishing industry. Turn left here, then left again to the limestone hump of **Humphrey Head**, jutting well into the Bay, and supposedly the place where the last wolf in England was killed. Cars may be parked on the beach and the headland makes a fine little stroll with views over the Bay. There is a cave and the'holy well of St Agnes Water', said to be good for rheumatism, gout and bilious complaints.

Return to Flookborough and drive through Cark. In 1km (0.6 mile) after Cark is **Holker Hall**, an early 16th-century mansion, now home of the Cavendish family and a major visitor attraction. In addition to the hall itself, there is a noted motor museum, birds of prey centre and award winning gardens. Special exhibitions and events such as a Garden and Countryside Festival.

Holker Hall

Picnic area; adventure playground; café; gift shop. Basic charge for gardens and deer park; extra charges for hall, motor museum and birds of prey centre. Open daily, except Saturdays, from late March to the end of October, 10.00–18.00 (last admissions 16.30). House closes 16.30. ☎ 015395 58328

Left & opposite: Holker Hall

Return to Cark and turn left, shortly reaching **Cartmel**, a delightful small town or big village centred on a compact square, with old inns, cafés and bookshops tightly clustered. Pride of place goes to **Cartmel Priory**, more than 800 years old. When the former priory was dissolved by King Henry VIII after 1537, the villagers managed to retain

the nave as their parish church, very grand indeed for such a modest sized place. Look out for the bullet holes in an external door, dating from the civil war (1643). Inside this light and lofty church there are many interesting features, notably the Cavendish family memorial and a Holy Family by Josefina de Vasconcellos of Ambleside.

In the Square, dominated by the former Priory gatehouse (National Trust – exhibitions), look out for the old fish dressing slabs and the remains of the old market cross. Car parking is at the edge of the **racecourse**, one of the smallest in the country, with meetings in late May and late August each year.

Cartmel Racecourse ☎ 015393 33434

Cartmel Show

Held on the Wednesday after the first Monday in August.
☎ 015397 22777

A minor road to the north from Cartmel leads to A590 1.5km (1 mile) south-east of Newby Bridge.

Fact File

REACHING THE LAKE DISTRICT

By car

Despite the restricted car parking and the limited network of predominantly narrow roads, the majority of visitors will arrive by car. The M6 motorway is the obvious approach road, from both north and south. From the south, junction 36, followed by the A590 and A591 provides a swift and straightforward approach to destinations in the south of the district. From the north east, the A66 is the best trans-Pennine route, crossing to Penrith from its junction with the A1 at Scotch Corner and then M6 south to junction 36. From the southern part of Yorkshire, the A65 via Skipton (bypassed) is the straightforward route.

By coach

Long distance coach is another option, generally less expensive than the railway. Stagecoach and National Express operate services to and from the Lake District from Birmingham, London, Manchester, South Yorkshire and the North-east, some passing through the heart of the district, calling at Kendal, Windermere, and Ambleside. These coaches serve many intermediate towns and cities throughout the country. Further information on these and local bus services, is available at Tourist Information Centres.

By rail

There is a west coast main line station at Oxenholme. From Oxenholme, the Windermere branch line provides a valuable service, generally with connections to and from the London (Euston) services, stopping at Kendal, Burneside, Staveley and Windermere. There are also through trains from Windermere to Manchester and its airport. National rail enquiries ☎ 0345 484950.

By air

The usual approach to the Lake District is by the international airport at Manchester. There are train services from the airport direct to Windermere and to Barrow in Furness.

ACCOMMODATION

Visitors will find accommodation to suit all needs and budgets, ranging from bunk houses and camping barns to luxury hotels; thousands of cottages and apartments are
also available to rent. Accommodation can always be
booked direct with the establishment or through a Tourist
Information Centre on or before arrival in the area. If reserved
through a T.I.C. a deposit of ten per cent will be charged; this will
be deducted when paying the final bill.
If calling personally, it is quite usual to ask to see the available
room at hotels or bed and breakfast houses.

Bunk Houses

Vary in character but offer clean, dry, very basic accommodation, sometimes in dormitories, at low cost. Some are situated in towns, others in rural areas. Current details obtainable from Tourist Information Centres.

Camping Barns

A network of stone barns, usually in remote places, owned by farmers but administered as a scheme by the Lake District National Park Authority (☎ 017687 72803 for reservations). The barns provide simple overnight shelter for walkers and cyclists, thus avoiding the need to carry tents. The only facilities are a wooden sleeping platform, table, cold water tap, and WC. Visitors will need to bring sleeping bags, cooking stove and accessories, and a torch. People under 18 years of age must be accompanied by an adult. Charges are very low.

Camping and Caravan Sites

Because of the impact on the landscape, many restrictions are imposed by the Lake District National Park Authority. Consequently most sites benefit from seclusion and are well screened from the roads and fells. Generally sites open only from mid-March to mid-November but exceptions do occur. Some sites have large static caravans and/or timber chalets to rent on a weekly (sometimes shorter) basis, as well as areas for touring caravans, motor caravans, and tents. Other sites will offer pitches exclusively for tourers and tents or one or the other. Farmers sometimes hold a local authority licence to use a small field for tents. The larger touring and camping sites are well equipped with showers, laundry, dish-washing and other facilities. Lists of sites can be obtained from Tourist Information Centres.

The two major clubs, the Caravan Club and the Camping and Caravanning Club own and manage sites in the area.

The Caravan Club has sites for touring caravans and motor caravans only, with one exception. It is possible for non-members to stay at all of these sites on payment of an increased over-night charge. The smaller certified location sites administered by the Caravan Club are licensed for members only and are limited to five vans per night; this type of site is frequently found to be a small field on a working farm and many do not have electric hook-ups or toilet facilities.

Details of membership, possible reciprocal arrangements with clubs in other countries and other information may be obtained from:

The Caravan Club
East Grinstead House
East Grinstead
RH19 1UA
☎ 01342 326944

The Camping and Caravanning Club
Greenfields House
Westwood Way
Coventry CV4 8JH
☎ 01203 694995

A Camping International Card, obtainable from caravan and camping clubs in many countries, may be useful.

Youth Groups

There are camp sites which cater for youth groups but reservation should be made well in advance of the proposed visit. Some of the churches provide dormitory accommodation in youth centres – again plan well ahead to ensure that the provision is suitable for the group concerned. Contact a Tourist Information Centre for more details.

Youth Hostels

The Youth Hostels Association has excellent coverage throughout the Lake District. The hostels, always very popular, vary from small buildings in the mountains to those of luxurious standard such as the one by the lake at Waterhead, Ambleside. It must be stressed that hostels are for travellers – young, not-so-young, solo, groups, school parties, families – all are welcome. Booking ahead is always advisable, and is essential for public holidays and in the peak season (July and August). Membership charges are modest – join on the spot at any hostel or write to:

Youth Hostels Association, Trevelyan House , 8 St Stephen's Hill, St Albans. AL1 2DY. ☎ 01727 845047

Membership includes the handbook listing all the hostels in England and Wales with the facilities offered and a location map.

The accommodation offered includes both family rooms and dormitories. Bedlinen is provided and included in the modest overnight charge. With few exceptions, all hostels provide meals, usually with a choice of menu and always a vegetarian option. Other diets can be catered for subject to advance notice. Charges for all meals are low and offer good value. All hostels provide a kitchen for those who prefer self-catering and all have a clothes drying facility, especially welcome to walkers and cyclists.

Subject to the availability of beds, there is no maximum or minimum length of stay.

Some hostels have a closed period during the day, usually 10.00–17.00. Doors are locked overnight, usually from 23.00.

With a few exceptions, all hostels can be reached by car and for those travelling by rail to the Lake District, the YHA runs a shuttle mini-bus (summer service only) from Windermere Station to local hostels.

Cottages, Flats and Residential Caravans

There are numerous agents who will offer a choice of accommodation to rent on a weekly basis or sometimes for even shorter periods. The size of the property, its facilities, and the cost will vary considerably. It is also possible to rent properties directly from the owner; these are advertised in the weekend newspapers, magazines such as *The Lady, Cumbria, Cumbria Life*; many are listed in booklets obtainable from Tourist Information Offices.

Some Agencies and Associations:

**Heart of the Lakes
and Cottage Life**
☎ 015394 32321 fax 33251

Cumbrian Cottages
☎ 015394 88772 fax 88902

Lakelovers
☎ 015394 88855 fax 88857

**Windermere Lake
District Holidays**
☎ 015394 43627

**Cumbria and Lakeland
Self-Caterers Association**
☎ (brochure) 0345 585199
fax 01229 861090
(vacancy advisory service)
☎ 015395 58153

Bed and Breakfast

Accommodation is offered in private houses or small proprietor-run guest houses in the towns, villages, or rural areas. Standards will vary and this is usually reflected in the price. Look for the B & B sign outside – some will quote the price; otherwise enquire at the door. Most offer at least some rooms with en-suite accommodation and a good standard of cleanliness. The majority do not serve meals other than breakfast but will be able to suggest good local restaurants to suit all budgets. Some of these guest houses will have a residents' lounge; almost all will provide tea and coffee facilities and television in the bedrooms. Remember, you can ask to see the room offered before accepting the accommodation.

Farmhouse Accommodation

Generally similar to the type offered above but in houses attached to working farms. Find addresses from T.I.C.s or guides widely available. Again standards will vary from simple to quite luxurious. Other than breakfast, meals if available, will sometimes be taken round a large table with the family and other guests. Some farmers will welcome visits to look round the farm and perhaps allow guests to help with the feeding of livestock.

Country House Hotels

The buildings are usually large houses in extensive grounds. Architecture and decor is frequently deluxe and service attentive. Such hotels usually have a tranquil setting with attractive views of mountains and/or lakes from the main rooms and from some of the bedrooms. It is customary to reserve a room, breakfast, and evening meal at this type of hotel.

Major and Large Hotels

Throughout the area there are many highly rated hotels. Most offer all the services expected from international hotels. As well as the restaurant, less formal eating areas such as the bar will offer meals and room service is available. Swimming pools and gymnasium facilities are also available in most hotels of this standard and most will cater for private parties and conferences.

The following establishments are merely suggestions from the large numbers available. More comprehensive information is available at Tourist Information Centres.

MAJOR AND LARGE HOTELS

The Castle Green Hotel
Kendal
☎ 01539 734000 fax 735522

Stonecross Manor Hotel
Kendal
☎ 01539 733559 fax 736386

Belsfield Hotel
Bowness on Windermere
☎ 015394 42448 fax 46397

Burnside Hotel
Bowness on Windermere
☎ 015394 42211 fax 43824

The Old England Hotel
Bowness on Windermere
☎ 015394 42444 fax 43432

Low Wood Hotel
Ambleside Road, Windermere
☎ 015394 33338 fax 34072

The Miller Howe Hotel
Windermere
☎ 015394 42536

Rothay Manor Hotel
Ambleside
☎ 015394 33605 fax 33607

Swan Hotel
Grasmere
☎ 015394 35551 fax 35741

Wordsworth Hotel
Grasmere
☎ 015394 35592 fax 35765

**Langdale Hotel and
Country Club**
Elterwater, Ambleside
☎ 0500 051197 fax 37694

Prince of Wales
Grasmere

COUNTRY HOUSE AND SMALLER HOTELS

Garden House Hotel
Fowl-Ing Lane, Kendal
☎ 01539 731131 fax 740064

Burn How Hotel
Back Belsfield Road,
Bowness on Windermere
☎ 015394 46226 fax 47000

Fayrer Garden Hotel
Lyth Valley Road,
Bowness on Windermere
☎ 015394 88195 fax 45986

Linthwaite House Hotel
Crook Road,
Bowness on Windermere
☎ 015394 88600 fax 88601

Quarry Garth Hotel
Ambleside Road, Windermere
☎ 015394 88282 fax 46584

Merewood Hotel
Ambleside Road, Windermere
☎ 015394 46484 fax 42128

Rothay Garth Hotel
Rothay Road, Ambleside
☎ 015394 32217 fax 34400

Wateredge Hotel
Waterhead, Ambleside
☎ 015394 32332 fax 31878

Nanny Brow Hotel
Clappersgate, Ambleside
☎ 015394 32036 fax 32450

Skelwith Bridge Hotel
Skelwith Bridge,
Ambleside
☎ 015394 32115 fax 34254

Gold Rill Hotel
Grasmere
☎/fax 015394 35486

Grasmere Hotel
Grasmere
☎/fax 015394 35277

Britannia Inn
Elterwater
☎ 015394 37210 fax 37311

New Dungeon Ghyll Hotel
Great Langdale
☎ 015394 37213

Old Dungeon Ghyll Hotel
Great Langdale
☎ 015394 37272

Three Shires Inn
Little Langdale
☎ 015394 37215

The Black Bull Inn
Coniston
☎ 015394 41335 fax 41168

The Sun Hotel
Coniston
☎ 015394 41248

The Waterhead Hotel
Coniston
☎ 015394 41244 fax 41193

Queen's Head Hotel
Hawkshead
☎ 015394 36271 fax 36722

Red Lion Inn
Hawkshead
☎ 015394 36213 fax 36747

Tower Bank Arms
Near Sawrey
☎ 015394 36334

Sawrey Hotel
Far Sawrey
☎ 015394 43425

AGRICULTURAL SHOWS, LOCAL SPORTS AND FESTIVALS

Westmorland County Show
 Kendal   ☎ 015395 67804

Lake District Sheepdog Trials
 Ings, Staveley   ☎ 015394 33721

Ambleside Sports   ☎ 015394 45531

Rydal Sheepdog Trials   ☎ TIC

Grasmere Sports   ☎ 015394 32127

Hawkshead Show   ☎ 015394 36609

Lowick Show   ☎ 015394 36364

BALLOON FLIGHTS

High Adventure
Bowness on Windermere   ☎ 015394 46588

CAR HIRE

Avis
Station Road, Kendal ☎ 01539 733582 and
Belsfield Garage,
Bowness on Windermere 015394 45910

Ford Rent-a-Car
Lakeland Ford, Mintsfeet Road South,
Mintsfeet Industrial Estate, Kendal ☎ 01539 723534

Vickers Self Drive
75, Appleby Road, Kendal ☎ 01539 732643

Rayrigg Rover
Shap Road, Kendal ☎ 01539 730060 and
Rayrigg Road, Windermere 015394 42451

Mint Motors
Mintsfeet Road, Kendal ☎ 01539 72333

Cumbria Car Hire Ltd
Troutbeck Bridge Service Station,
Windermere ☎ 015394 44408
fax 015394 42200

CYCLE HIRE

Daisy Cycle Hire
Craig Walk,
Bowness on Windermere ☎ 015394 42144

Bike Hire
46, Oak Street, Windermere ☎ 015394 48031

Mountain Trading
Lake Road, Bowness ☎ 015394 44786

David Ashton
Elleray Hotel, Cross Street,
Windermere ☎ 015394 43120

Ambleside Mountain Bikes
The Slack, Ambleside ☎ 015394 33592

Biketreks
Millans Park, Ambleside ☎ 015394 31245

Lakes Pathfinders
Ambleside ☎ 015394 32862
(0374 167 695)

The Croft Mountain Bike Hire
Hawkshead   ☎ 015394 36374

Grizedale Mountain Bikes
Grizedale   ☎ 01229 860369

Crook Barn Stables
Torver, Coniston   ☎ 015394 41088

Summitreks
Yewdale Road, Coniston   ☎ 015394 41212

Meadowdore Cafe
Coniston   ☎ 015394 41638.

There is a waymarked mountain bike route at Grizedale
Forest. Details at the forest visitor centre.

Note

· Byways (usually unsurfaced roads) are open to cyclists,
  horseriders and walkers; off-road vehicles may also be
  encountered.
· Bridleways are open to cyclists but horseriders and walkers have
  right of way.
· Footpaths are **not** available to cyclists.
· Open land – there is no right of access for cyclists on fells or
  farmland without the permission of the landowner.
· Always comply with the *Mountain Biking Code of Conduct.*

EATING OUT

All the large hotels and the majority of the country house and
smaller hotels will provide meals for non-residents, though
sometimes only in the evening. Almost all inns provide bar food
both at mid-day and in the evening.
The following list adds futher suggestions for each section of the
district, ranging from expensive, high quality, restaurants to more
simple premises including tea and coffee shops not open in the
evening.
  An exceptional restaurant, worthy of separate mention, is:

The Miller Howe Hotel, Windermere, ☎ 015394 42536

Déjà Vu   **Duffins Restaurant**
124 Stricklandgate. Kendal   54 Stramongate, Kendal
☎ 01539 724843   ☎ 01539 720387

Farrers Tea and Coffee Shop
13 Stricklandgate, Kendal
☎ 01539 731707

Paulo Gianni's
21a Stramongate, Kendal
☎ 01539 725858

Waterside Wholefoods
Kent View, Kendal
☎ 01539 729743

Magic Wok
2 Crescent Road, Windermere
☎ 015394 88668

Jericho's
Birch Street, Windermere
☎ 015394 42522

Renoirs Coffee Shop
Main Street, Windermere
☎ 015394 44863

Roger's
4 High Street, Windermere
☎ 015394 44954

Bowness Kitchen
Lake Road, Bowness
☎ 015394 45529

The Porthole
Ash Street, Bowness
☎ 015394 42793

Rastelli's
Lake Road, Bowness
☎ 015394 44227

The Spinnery Restaurant
Kendal Road, Bowness
☎ 015394 42756

Trattoria Ticino
Quarry Rigg, Bowness
☎ 015394 45786

Ambles Brasserie
Lake Road, Ambleside
☎ 015394 33970

Bertrams Restaurant
Market Place, Ambleside
☎ 015394 32119

Dodds Restaurant
Rydal Road, Ambleside
☎ 015394 32134

The Cumbria Carvery
Stock Lane, Grasmere
☎ 015394 35005

Langman's Tea Shop
Stock Lane, Grasmere
☎ 015394 35248

Rowan Tree Vegetarian Restaurant
Stock Lane, Grasmere
☎ 015394 35528

Kirkstone Gallery
Skelwith Bridge
☎ 015394 32553

The Wine Restaurant
Coniston
☎ 015394 41256

The Minstrel's Gallery
Hawkshead
☎ 015394 36423

Whigs
The Square, Hawkshead
☎ 015394 36614

The Café
Grizedale Visitor Centre, Grizedale
☎ 01229 860011

Boater's Restaurant
Lakeside, Newby Bridge
☎ 015395 31381

Fell Foot Park Café
Newby Bridge
☎ 015395 31273

FACILITIES FOR THE DISABLED

Where possible, an indication of facilities available at individual attractions has been made in the text. General guidance about facilities, including a list of public toilets in the area with wheelchair access, can be obtained from Cumbria Tourist Board. ☎ 015394 44444.

FISHING

An Environment Agency rod licence must be purchased by anyone wishing to fish in any water in England. (North-west region, North Area headquarters, ☎ 01228 25151). The licence is available from post offices and tourist information centres. In addition, a permit must be obtained from the Angling Association or riparian owner owning the fishing rights. However, in the Lake District, certain lakes and tarns may be fished by rod licence holders without additional permit, either from a shore where there is public access or from a boat on lakes or tarns where launching is permitted.

Windermere

Alcock Tarn, Grasmere
Easdale Tarn, Grasmere
Grisedale Tarn, Grasmere
Codale Tarn, Grasmere

Coniston Water

Levers Water, Coniston
Goats Water Coniston
High Dam, Finsthwaite

Of the above, Windermere has the greatest variety of fish, including the rare and highly esteemed char. The smaller tarns are generally limited to brown trout, with perch and schelly present in a minority of cases.

A useful leaflet, *Fishing in Lakeland*, produced by Windermere, Ambleside and District Angling Association, is available from tourist information offices.

GOLF

Kendal (pro)   ☎ 01539 723499

Carus Green, Burneside   ☎ 01539 721097

Windermere (pro)   ☎ 015394 43550

GUIDED TOURS

Cumbria Tourist Guides (Association of Registered Blue Badge Guides), Mickle Bower, Temple Sowerby, Penrith, CA10 1RZ. ☎ 017683 62233; fax 017683 62211

Nearly 50 qualified 'Blue Badge' guides are listed as available to provide a wide variety of guided tours for visitors. All are experienced in general guiding in the district; additionally, many have areas of particular expertise such as local literature, gardens or religious monuments. Mini-buses and/or motor cars may be provided by the guides. Several languages are spoken.

Mountain Goat Tours and Holidays
Windermere, Bowness, Ambleside and Grasmere
☎ 015394 45161 fax 015394 45164

Lakes Supertours, Windermere ☎ 015394 88133

Lakeland Safari Tours Windermere
Bowness, Ambleside and Grasmere ☎ 015394 33904

National Trust full and half-day Lake District Landscape Tours by minibus ☎ 015394 35599 or tourist information centres.

Princess Executive Minicoaches, Kendal ☎ 01539 731894

GUIDED WALKS

Lake District National Park Authority
Brockhole, Windermere. ☎ 015394 45555
An extensive programme of guided walks is available throughout the year, generally led by a Voluntary Warden, from many centres throughout the district. 'Discovery Walks', with a theme, are led by experts in their particular field. Voluntary Warden walks are free but a modest charge is made for Discovery Walks. Walks are graded easy, moderate or strenuous. The full programme is included in the National Park publication *Events*, produced annually.

South Lakeland Guided Walks – Town, Village and Country
A comprehensive programme of walks exploring the towns and villages of the southern part of the district, organised by South Lakeland District Council. Based on the various Tourist Information Centres in most cases. A modest charge is made. Telephone Tourist Information Centres for details.

Countrywide, Forest Side, Grasmere. ☎ 015394 35250

Loughrigg Brow, Ambleside. ☎ 015394 32229
A charge is made.

HORSE RIDING

Hipshow Riding Stables
Kendal   ☎ 01539 728221

Holmescale Riding Centre
Kendal   ☎ 01539 729388

Larkrigg Riding School
Kendal   ☎ 015395 60245

Tarnside Trekking
Lyth Valley   ☎ 015395 68288

Lakeland Equestrian
Windermere   ☎ 015394 43811

Rydal Farm Trekking
Rydal   ☎ 015394 34131
(0850 102721)

Ellergarth Riding
Langdale   ☎ 015394 37274

Crook Barn
Coniston   ☎ 015394 41088

Spoon Hall Trekking Centre
Coniston   ☎ 015394 41391

Bigland Hall Estate
Newby Bridge   ☎ 015395 31728

MAPS

The following Ordnance Survey maps cover the areas included in this book. The use of the appropriate map is advised when following the walks, cycle rides or car tours.

Landranger 90 *Penrith & Keswick, Ambleside* 1:50,000

Landranger 96 *Barrow-in-Furness & South Lakeland* 1:50,000

Landranger 97 *Kendal & Morecambe* 1:50,000

Outdoor Leisure 5 *The English Lakes – North Eastern Area* 1:25,000

Outdoor Leisure 6 *The English Lakes – South Western Area* 1:25,000

Outdoor Leisure 7 *The English Lakes – South Eastern Area* 1:25,000

NATURE RESERVES

Cumbria Wildlife Trust produce a brochure *Nature Reserves in Cumbria* listing 33 reserves throughout the county.
The majority of these are not in the Lake District but could readily be included in a motor car or cycle tour.
Those actually in the district are:

Ash Landing, close to Far Sawrey. G.R. 386954.

Dorothy Farrers Spring Wood, near Staveley.
  G.R. 480983.

Hervey Reserve (Whitbarrow) Access at G.R. 436859.

Latterbarrow, near Witherslack village.
  G.R. (car park) 441827.

PUBLIC TRANSPORT IN THE AREA

The Cumbria County Council operates a 'Journey Planner' information and enquiry service for bus, rail and boat timetables at Citadel Chambers, Carlisle, Cumbria CA3 8SG. ☎ 01228 606000 (Monday to Friday 9.00–1700 Saturday 9.00–12.00,)

   Journey Planner on the Internet, visit the website at www.cumbria.gov.uk

   The following leaflets detailing public transport services in the area are available from tourist information centres and Cumbria County Council:

   Getting Around Cumbria and the Lake District

   Lakeland Explorer

   To and Through Cumbria and the Lake District

   Handy Guide to Buses and Boats in Central Lakeland

Stagecoach Cumberland
☎ 01946 63222

The National Trust Bus

The National Trust runs a free minibus shuttle between Hawkshead and Coniston, via Tarn Hows, on Sundays between April and the end of October. This links to the timetable of the steam yacht Gondola on Coniston.
☎ 015394 35599.

SMALLER HOUSES OPEN TO THE PUBLIC

Townend, Troubeck
(National Trust)   ☎ 015394 32628

Rydal Mount, Rydal   ☎ 015394 33002

Dove Cottage, Grasmere   ☎ 015394 35544 (daytime)
015394 35651 (evenings)

Hill Top, Near Sawrey
(National Trust)   ☎ 015394 36269

Brantwood, Coniston   ☎ 015394 41396

STATELY HOMES OPEN TO THE PUBLIC

Sizergh Castle, Sizergh,
Kendal (National Trust.)   ☎ 015395 60070

Levens Hall, Levens   ☎ 015395 60321

Holker Hall, Cark in Cartmel   ☎ 015395 58328

Leighton Hall, near Carnforth   ☎ 01524 734474

TOURIST BOARD

Cumbria Tourist Board, Ashleigh, Holly Road, Windermere
☎ 015394 44444

TOURIST INFORMATION CENTRES

Kendal, Town Hall   ☎ 01539 725758

Windermere, Victoria Street   ☎ 015394 46499

***Bowness**, Bowness Bay   ☎ 015394 42895

Brockhole, Windermere
(National Park)   ☎ 015394 46601

***Waterhead**, The Car Park   ☎ 015394 32729

Ambleside, opposite new
new shopping mall   ☎ 015394 32582

***Grasmere**, Red Bank Road   ☎ 015394 35245

*__Hawkshead__, main car park ☎ 015394 36525

__Coniston__, main car park,
Ruskin Avenue ☎ 015394 41533

*_Either closed or limited opening hours out of season._

WATER SPORTS AND OTHER ACTIVITIES

__Lake Holidays Afloat__
Glebe Road, Bowness ☎ 015394 43415

__Pleasure in Leisure__
Arrangement of many types of holiday activity, including water sports, mountaineering, caving, archery, pony-trekking, pigeon shooting, paragliding, traditional sports, car hire. ☎ 015394 42324

__Windermere Outdoor Adventure Watersports Centre__
Rayrigg Road ☎ 015394 47183

__Spirit of the Lake__
Shepherd's Boatyard, Windermere ☎ 015394 48322

__Maples__
Marina Village, Windermere ☎ 0539 773292 or 015395 30063

__Sport Aquatic__
Windermere Quays Visitor Centre ☎ 015394 42121

__Low Wood Water Sports Centre__
south of Waterhead, Windermere ☎ 015394 33338

__Coniston Boating Centre__ ☎ 015394 41366

__Summitreks__
Coniston ☎ 015394 41212
fax 015394 41089

WEATHER

Lakes Weather Line ☎ 017687 75757

INDEX

LANDMARK
Publishing Ltd ● ● ● ●

VISITORS GUIDES

* Practical guides for the independent traveller
* Written in the form of touring itineraries
* Full colour illustrations and maps
* Detailed Landmark FactFile of practical information
* Landmark Visitors Guides highlight all the interesting places you will want to see, so ensuring that you make the most of your visit

1. *Britain*
   Cornwall
   Cotswolds &
     Shakespeare
     Country
   Devon
   Dorset
   East Anglia
   Guernsey
   Hampshire
   Jersey
   Lake District
   Peak District
   Scotland
   Somerset
   Yorkshire Dales
     & York

LANDMARK VISITORS GUIDE
Lake District
Norman Buckley

2. *Europe*
   Bruges
   Cracow
   Italian Lakes
   Madeira
   Provence
   Riga
   Tallinn

"One of the best Lake District walking guide books I have seen" – G Armstrong, Editor, East Yorkshire & Derwent Area Rambling Association. **Over 60 walks on more than 40 A4 maps around and between youth hostels. Ideal even if you are staying in a nearby hotel!** *INCLUDES A FREE YHA MEMBERSHIP VOUCHER WORTH £10.* ISBN No 1-901522-26 1, 192 pages, £7.99

3. *Other*
   Dominican Republic
   Florida: Gulf Coast
   Florida Keys
   India: Goa
   India: Kerala
     & The South
   New Zealand
   Orlando &
     Central Florida
   St Lucia
   The Gambia

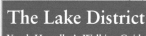

The Lake District
Youth Hosteller's Walking Guide

Martyn Hanks

INC: FREE YHA MEMBERSHIP

Landmark Publishing
Waterloo House, 12 Compton, Ashbourne, Derbyshire DE6 IDA England
Tel: 01335 347349 Fax: 01335 347303 e-mail: landmark@clara.net
Catalogue sent on request

Published by
Landmark Publishing Ltd,
Waterloo House, 12 Compton, Ashbourne, Derbyshire DE6 1DA England
Tel: 01335 347349 Fax: 01335 347303 e-mail: landmark@clara.net

1st Edition
ISBN 1 901 522 53 9

© **Norman Buckley 1999**

The right of Norman Buckley as author of this work has been asserted by him in
accordance with the Copyright, Design and Patents Act, 1993.

British Library Cataloguing in Publication Data: a catalogue record for this book
is available from the British Library.

Print: UIC Printing & Packaging Pte Ltd, Singapore
Cartography & Design: Samantha Witham
Editor: Kay Coulson

Front Cover: Rydal Fell and Grasmere from the lake shore path
Back cover, top: Lengthening shadows at the
end of the day by Little Langdale Tarn;
Back cover, bottom: Shepherds sticks for sale at the
Sheep Dog Trials, Rydal

Picture Credits:
Lindsey Porter: Front cover, back cover top, 3, 5, 19, 22, 25, 26, 27 both,
30, 32, 33, 36, 37, 38, 39, 42, 43, 46, 48, 51, 52, 53, 54, 55, 57, 59 both,
60, 66, 69, 71 both, 74, 76, 77

Norman Buckley: Back cover bottom, 10, 14, 16, 21,
28, 29 both, 61, 62 both, 65

June Buckley: 13, 63